# InScribed

InScribe Christian Writers' Fellowship

# InScribed

## 30 Years of Inspiring Writers

forever books
WINNIPEG, CANADA
www.foreverbooks.ca

InScribed



ISBN: 978-1-926718-20-0

Cover Design: Yvonne Parks Design
Book Design: Andrew Mackay
Managing Editor: Rick Johnson



Published by

Forever Books

Winnipeg Canada

www.foreverbooks.ca

# Contents

*Contents*

# Introduction

THIRTY YEARS OF INSPIRING Writing. The subtitle says it all.

Having been associated with InScribe for almost that long, I can attest to the fact that the group does indeed include both inspiring and inspired writers and those who teach them. I've had the privilege of being on both sides of that coin, learning from those who have reached a level of excellence by honing their talents and then passing on the skills and tricks of the trade I have learned along the way.

It has been a joy and a vital link to the amazing creativity and grace of God as I've associated with these writers, watched them bloom and grow and marvelled at what God has done. It's been a thrill to get to know writers who are not striving after fame and gain but who are working for the Kingdom of God all across the country, from the islands off the coast of B.C. to the shores of the Atlantic and the northern territories. In a country so vast, the web of connection by internet, satellite groups and annual conferences has been vital to the growth of the organization. That web has been a big part of my journey from a "wannabe" to a published author.

It has also been a privilege to serve on the executive committee in various capacities, joining a group of people not only talented in writing but also in administration. Their dedication and joy in Christ (evidenced by much laughter at our regular meetings) often spilled over into my life and left me changed. I owe them all a debt I could never repay, for their friendship, their commitment to the call to write and dedication to training and empowering writers of faith.

So it is with great satisfaction, pleasure and gratitude that I see this anthology come to be, a true celebration of InScribe Christian Writers' Fellowship and a true testimony to God's glory.

Sincerely,

Marcia Laycock
*author of One Smooth Stone, A Tumbled Stone, Spur of the Moment and Focussed Reflections.*

WHEN I FIRST STUMBLED ACROSS InScribe, they were in the midst of another anniversary celebration: their twentieth. It's hard to believe that I've been a part of this incredible organization for that long. As I look back, I can credit InScribe with a large part of how much I've learned and grown as a writer in the last ten years.

One thing that InScribe has taught me is to give back. Writers are an incredibly generous, friendly group of people, always willing to share what they have learned. As so many writers have helped me, I have tried to help others. I've come to realize that writing is a journey: there will always be someone further ahead on the road who is willing to help me and someone further back on the road whom I can help.

I love going to conferences and talking to writers I saw a year ago at the last conference, and hearing what they've done since then. It's always fun to see the contest winners and get a taste of what fellow InScribers are writing. So I was very excited about this project—the chance for us to showcase our work and to encourage each other by showing what we've been writing. As I read through the submissions, I found myself amazed by the talent in this group. I hope you will enjoy reading these selections of the InScribe Christian Writers' Fellowship as much as the editors have.

Bonnie Way,
*editor, freelance writer, blogger*

AND NOW A BIT ABOUT THE selection process. Nothing has made me more pragmatic about my own acceptances and rejections than being involved in judging contests and working on the selection committee for various magazines and anthologies. Where two or three are gathered, there are two or three opinions. Each of us compiled individual short lists, and differences between those lists were discussed between us, and not without prayer. I am confident that the book you hold in your hands is as rich in variety and writing quality as possible.

Enjoy!

Susan Plett,
*mother, wife, writer, editor, dogwalker*

# *Strange Attractor*

Stephen T. Berg

WHEN I WAS BOY, ARMED WITH wire cutters, a screwdriver, and a soldering iron, I would happily pass evenings and weekends tearing apart—and sometimes putting back together—discarded radios or anything else I found that ran on batteries or had to be plugged in. I loved the smell of solder and gave myself headaches soldering together crude circuits consisting of resistors, switches, relays, capacitors and transformers.

For a while I had a fling with solenoids or electromagnets. The first one I made had snare wire wrapped tightly around a two inch nail. I hooked the two ends to a six volt battery and as the current fled through the wire it produced an electromagnetic field and magnetized the nail. In the effort to pick up increasingly heavier metal objects, I went on to bigger and better versions. One day I built a very fine one that required being plugged into an outlet. Although I used a step-down transformer between the power source and the electromagnet, I miscalculated and it blew up sending bits of hot wire flying across my bedroom and burning holes in my shirt.

Still, I was seized by the magic of creating an instant magnetic field. I marveled that a cold dead nail could suddenly pulse with an invisible power. And I was fascinated that the immaterial field that was created around this simple object, reoriented and brought into alignment everything in its range.

I recall all of this only because one evening following a Wednesday night gathering, my wife, Deb, told me about an impression she experienced. That evening our friend Mary had offered Deb her chair beside the fireplace so she could warm herself. Deb told me that when she sat in Mary's chair she felt a soft peace coming over her; and it came to her that this was the place where Mary prayed.

This brings me to wonder about the parallel natures of my electromagnet and the *prayer-chair* by the fire place. I wonder about Deb being affected by an unseen field of influence where things were brought into alignment in such a way that a subtle profusion of peace was the result. I wonder how far I can take the notion that a place of prayer, a person of prayer, a prayer itself, brings harmony and peace to its surroundings.

In an essay called *The Physics of Communion*, Barbara Taylor talks about an experience she had at a lecture given by Fred Burnham. Burnham is an Episcopal priest who holds a doctorate in the history of science. The lecture was about chaos theory and the science of complexity, and how these things might begin to inform religion. During the lecture a computer screen was left on; random lines crisscrossed the screen. By the end of the lecture the lines had produced a striking facsimile of a butterfly. Burnham called the butterfly design a "strange attractor" because the mathematical formula that created the design acted like a magnet that pulled randomness into form and order.

The experience my wife had is of course beyond scientific examination, but perhaps at some undiscovered level, the equating of the *prayer-chair* with an electromagnet does not violate science or faith. Perhaps only those of us who have yet to completely shed a mechanistic world view find difficulty with this juxtaposition. To those that see the created world as God's world—as in, "God is over all and through all and in all" (Ephesians 4:6 NIV).—there will be awe and wonder, but no incredulity; because at bottom, the spiritual and the material natures are not distinct categories.

If this is the way things are, should it surprise us that the chair beside the fireplace is hallowed ground? Should it surprise us that this spot has become a place where an invisible power, through the conducting rays of prayer, however prayed, however fashioned, realigns and reorders that which is in range?

Perhaps this helps us better reverence those times we remember being arrested by a power that we could only call holy. Nothing planned or invented, we were simply held entranced in space and time, held together in a way that suspended all our fears. We were in a field of holy influence, where God, for no reason or a thousand reasons, chose to stream Divine love into the world through an old shed, a tree, a butterfly, a path, a café, a stranger, a friend. Could these be revelatory ruptures, unifying moments, meant to lead us deeper and transform our false autonomy into true attractiveness?

While deep mystery remains, we can still catch the notion that when we allow the *current* of Christ to flow through us, not impeding it or attempting to store it, just letting it flow freely, as happens in honest prayer, we too become strange attractors, carrying within us and around us, beauty and order.

And we find we carry it even more fully and beautifully and orderly when we carry it with others, where the *two or more* are gathered. Through the church, wherever the few are gathered, the fallen *powers and principalities* that scripture describes as being created in and for Christ are reoriented, redeemed, and recreated to their original design and for their original purpose—that of serving Christ.

At this revelatory juncture the possibilities seem boundless. Consider the church a strange attractor, moving through chaos, aligning the powers, reorienting the principalities, bringing coherence and peace in its wake.

Is this too fanciful? Perhaps not fanciful enough. It is, after all, Christ that makes this a creative possibility, "He is before all things, and in him all things hold together" (Colossians 1:17 NIV). The presence of Christ in each one of us make us all strange attractors—makes us parts of the body of the Grand Strange Attractor.

# Kolya

Janice L. Dick

HE SAT ON THE EDGE OF A kitchen chair, forehead creased in concentration, and strummed his old guitar. His song alternated between vocals and occasional accompaniment on the harmonica fitted into a wire brace around his neck.

"Keep on the sunny side, always on the sunny side," he wailed, his voice gravelly from years of pipe smoke and loud conversation. His eyes twinkled as he grinned at me.

At nine years of age, I found him strangely charming. Even my younger sister, shy of most everyone, sat comfortably on his knee at the end of this impromptu concert.

Uncle Nick's visits always proved exciting to us kids. His death-grip handshake and hearty greeting of, "So how are ya brats?" still makes me smile. I can still smell his tobacco-seasoned breath, see his grey eyes dancing with mischief and delight. His true spirit was as obvious as the fat cigar clenched mercilessly between yellowed teeth.

Through the years, I came to expect the unexpected from his rare visits.

"You drive my car," he said to me as he climbed into the passenger door of the steel grey, late model Cadillac.

My sixteen-year-old confidence faltered.

"C'mon, Kid!" he hollered through the window. "You got

your license, ain't ya?"

He grinned broadly as I sat behind the wheel and turned the key in the ignition. He had more faith in me than I had in myself as we wound down through the hills and across the Oldman River on the single lane Nolan Bridge. This was, however, not his most momentous river crossing.

"Yup, me and your dad swum this creek on horseback when we was about your age," he reminisced. "Your dad's sister Tina's brother-in-law had just drowned trying to cross the river.

"The man was afraid of water. Lost his grip on his horse and got sucked down by one of them undertows. A man won't drown if he hangs onto his horse. Me and your dad and our friend Pete, we decided to prove that fact."

Uncle Nick jammed his pipe between his teeth and proceeded to light it.

"So here's a lesson for ya." He winked and pointed at me with his pipe. "Never let go of your horse."

"Yes, Sir."

"It was as fine a day as you could want. Just a few of them swirly clouds, at least to start with. We boys were itchin' for adventure."

He continued to paint a colorful picture of what happened that summer of 1937 when they had crossed the river over and back. Nothing of import happened at the time, but they vowed not to breathe a word of their escapade to their parents, for fear of discipline. I had a feeling those three harbored other secrets from their elders, for everyone's benefit.

"It was difficult for Nick," my dad told me years later. "As long as his mother was alive, he was spared the brunt of his brothers' rough treatment, but she died while he was still young. Nick suffered the most, and I guess he learned to act tough to cover up."

Nicholai Enns was born in South Russia during the turbulent post-revolution days of the early 1920s. His parents, along with thousands of other Mennonites, emigrated with their families to Canada. Kolya, as he was known by his family, was only three or four years of age at the time of the journey. He grew up loud and tough.

His first marriage ended after less than two years. A second attempt lasted many years and produced two children, but it was a strange, strained relationship and did not endure. In the end, he gave up on conventional marriage and opted for companionship with a feisty German woman named Ingrid. She told us of his latest faux pas when we paid a rare visit to his home in British Columbia.

"No sense in his head," said Ingrid, affection coloring her words.

"Oh, stop fussing, Woman!" he said, grimacing as he lifted his bandaged leg onto a weathered footstool.

We waited for explanation.

"I was cuttin' down trees in the woods." His voice crackled as he met my eyes. "One of them dang logs rolled my way, nearly killed me. Caused this huge blister on the back of my leg. My jackknife was pretty clean so I wiped the blade on my jeans and lanced the blister right then and there."

I winced. His jeans were filthy even now.

"Crazy old man," Ingrid said. "If not for me and the doctor, you would not have that leg anymore. Three months and it only starts to heal."

"Oh, you never mind," Uncle Nick retorted. "I'm still livin', ain't I?"

I stood to examine the photographs lining the fireplace mantle. He limped over and pointed to one.

"Looky here," he motioned me over. "This is Steve." A tanned, well-muscled young man squinted into the sun against a backdrop of craggy mountain peaks.

"My eldest grandson." His eyes misted and he cleared his throat. "He was killed last summer. Mountain climbing accident in Nepal. Government wouldn't even let us bring his body home."

Uncle Nick shook his head, pushed his hands deep into his pockets and stared at nothing out the window.

"Sure miss that boy," he sighed as he eased back into his chair.

I said goodbye to Uncle Nick with regret and a bear hug. I would see him alive only once more. He would play and sing "Keep on the Sunny Side" in memory of my father as I fought to retain my composure.

Then, at the end of his life, he would follow my dad's lead and turn himself over to the One who had been mercifully dogging him all his life. I imagine he hung onto his horse at that final river crossing, and then grinned as he shook off mortality to join up with John and Pete—and Jesus—on the sunny side.

# Make Time For Your Passion

Sharon Espeseth

MANY OF US HAVE HOBBIES OR activities we are passionate about: pet projects and pursuits that re-create us. When life is busy, we put our passions on the shelf. Often that is a high shelf in a deep closet.

For a while, we longingly think of our beloved projects and pine for that re-creative task. But then we pile more stuff on top of our painting, writing, quilting, or whatever it is we enjoy. We stack stuff in front of it. Feeling beaten by our inability to indulge our avocation, we try to forget the whole business.

It doesn't have to be like that. I believe God gives us these passions for a reason. These longings may well be gifts God wants us to use. He doesn't want us to bury our talents like the servant who hid his coin in the field.

My passion is writing. Yours may be painting, music, photography, or golfing. Considering our passion a gift or calling may make us more respectful of it and may encourage us to take time for its pleasure. When Jesus commanded us to love our neighbour as ourselves, he meant we should treat our neighbours *and* ourselves well. Does that mean he wants us to enjoy our God-given abilities?

At some points in our lives, we may have only short periods to devote to our special interest. Unless we clearly set our priorities, however, it is easy to fill that space with something else. Without neglecting our families or our jobs, can we squeeze in a short session each day, or an hour a week, to do something that lifts our spirits?

Although writing has long been my passion, for many years those minutes mostly meant scribbling in my journal. Even in retirement, busy days try to squeeze out writing. Procrastination, my old nemesis, still haunts me. Here I am at 65 with my brain chock-full of memories, knowledge, ideas, experience, skills, and passion—tools a writer needs.

Now as a late-bloomer, I accept this old proverb: "The best time to plant a tree was twenty years ago. The second best time is now." Since I began writing over twenty years ago, it is time to kick it up a notch. Chaucer said, "The lyf so short, the craft so long to lerne."

This year, after a long apprenticeship, I intend to elevate my craft to a higher level of importance in my life. Along with more precise goals, I will upgrade my work habits and attitudes. Qualities like faith, courage, determination, self-discipline, perseverance, and assertiveness come to mind. I have collected inspiring quotes from the combined wisdom of the Universe, including scripture.

Although I have ideas and skill, I still need focus, discipline, and courage. Clarifying my goals, I will press toward the mark. I need the psalmist's inspiration for a noble theme and Paul's self-discipline. As a generalist I do several things passably well: I cook. I sing. I knit. Now I need to adopt Paul's this-one-thing-I do philosophy.

Single-mindedness includes learning to say no. Like Martha in the New Testament, I've accepted jobs I feel I must. It's time I emulate Martha's sister, Mary, in choosing the better part. This requires wisdom and courage, which God will supply if I only ask. Paul advised Timothy that God did not give us a spirit of timidity, but a spirit of power, of love and self-discipline (2 Tim 1:7 NIV).

Wanting time to write, I now claim the courage, power, love, and self-discipline God offers. He can give me wisdom to be a better juggler of life's circumstances. Accepting God's lead, I'll know when to set the timer and write.

As for success, in Proverbs 16:3, we read that if we commit what we do to the Lord, our plans will succeed. T. S. Eliot said, "For us, there is only the trying. The rest is not our business." Wouldn't God agree?

Like David, I want to be aware of my life's end and the number of days remaining. (Psalm 39:4 NIV) Nevertheless, I don't want to be stymied by that awareness. Rather, I want to be spiritual enough to flourish like the palm trees and the cedars of Lebanon and to bring forth fruit in my old age.

Further inspiration can be gleaned from the achievements of well-known elderly folk. At 71, Michelangelo was painting the Sistine Chapel. Grandma Moses *began* painting after 80 and completed over 1500 paintings. Schweitzer was still performing surgery in his African hospital at 89.

We don't have to wait until we're 80 to be committed to our calling. George Eliot said, "It is never too late to be who you might have been." Scripture says, "To everything there is a season." This is my season to write. With God teaching me to number my days, I'll call today No. 1.

# Crossroad Epiphany

Mary Waind

*December 1, 1958*

THIS MUST BE IT – CORNER OF First Line West and Side Road 11. Professor Timothy Harris turned his loaded station wagon onto the gravel road and caught his first glimpse of the property.

No! Not a school!

The real estate agent hadn't said anything about a school on the land. He'd described a white stucco house, furnished, a barn, an orchard. How could that man have thought a school on an acre by the road not worth mentioning? Was it because he was moving in alone? The agent had said the chap who rented the fields would be coming and going and would plow the lane when it snowed, but no word about a schoolyard full of noisy children.

Two thirds of his sabbatical was gone. Only four months remained to complete his research and writing. He couldn't start searching for another place. Hopefully a series of brutal snowstorms would force the kids to stay in for recess, or, better yet, keep them home altogether.

Tim stopped in front of the garage. The agent had given him a house key. He hadn't said anything about getting into the garage, but Tim lifted the simple latch and pulled the two doors open. Good - plenty of room to park the station wagon inside out of the wind while he unloaded his luggage. The door from the garage to the kitchen wasn't locked either. Tim began to suspect the key might fit the front door which no one used. Perhaps locks weren't necessary here?

Pleasant warmth welcomed him. Someone had made sure the furnace was running. After a quick look through each room, Tim unpacked the groceries he'd picked up in the village. He lugged his two suitcases up the stairs and shoved them into the bedroom that faced the orchard.

He'd grabbed some lunch at the café in the village. It was already past two o'clock. Tim moved the kitchen table close to the bay window. He took his typewriter out of its case, set it on the table and began to sort his materials, arranging them across the wide surface. Concepts he'd mulled over as he drove began to connect. He attacked his task from a fresh perspective. This was going to work.

A loud knock startled Tim. Drat! He'd only been working for a couple of hours. Maybe if he stayed quiet in the dim room, whoever it was would think there was no one home.

Just then the door opened and a small girl stepped in. The hood of her plaid jacket slipped back to reveal tousled brown curls framing an inquisitive freckled face. She held a wicker basket with a blue checkered towel tucked over the contents. Tim decided locks were necessary and determined to turn the one on that door as soon as this little intruder left.

"Wow, Mr. Harris, it's getting dark. I couldn't see in the garage. You need some lights on."

Tim had barely managed to stand up.

The child flicked the light switch by the door, and stamped the snow off her boots on the mat.

"Now just a minute." Tim liked to be in control.

"I'm Bonnie, Mr. Harris, Bonnie Geddes. Am I supposed to call you 'Professor'?"

"Mr. Harris is fine, but…"

"Mommy made macaroni and cheese for supper. She said it might be hard for you to cook for yourself tonight when you just moved in. There are beets too. I don't like beets very much. Do you?" Bonnie set the small casserole and jar of beets on the counter.

"Well, I'm…"

"My Grandpa Geddes liked beets. This was his house. He died in September. I was sort of hoping you would be like a grandpa. Guess you aren't old enough to be a grandpa, are you?"

The bluster in Tim evaporated. He struggled not to smile.

"That's okay. You don't have to be a grandpa to come to our Christmas concert. We're having it in three weeks on Friday, at 1:00 o'clock. Mommy is our teacher. She makes our concerts fun. I'd better get going. She'll be ready to go home."

Since Julie's death twelve years earlier, the wound in Tim's heart festered most at Christmas. He'd planned to skip the season in this rural hideaway. That was before Bonnie plunged into his life. If he locked the kitchen door she tapped on the window. How could such a bright little thing not get it? In her mind the possibility that she was not welcome must not exist. Somehow she had gleaned more tenacity in her nine years than Tim had in his thirty-nine.

At one o'clock on the afternoon of December 19th, Tim squeezed into the back of the school room. Before long, he decided Bonnie was right. Her mommy's concerts were fun, for both the young performers and their guests. Tim was impressed – and even more so when the grown-up version of his small friend concluded her Christmas wishes to the audience.

"This is the second Christmas since Bonnie and I lost her father. I've always loved this season, but its message means more to me now. The One whose birth we celebrate has given me comfort and strength, even joy and hope for our future. May He do this for each of you."

Gently, a hint of these qualities began to seep into Tim's soul. Might he discover something better than a hideaway at the corner of First Line West and Side Road 11? The grin on a familiar freckled face gave him hope.

# The Novice and the Editor

Susan Roberts Plett

"THE ROUND BLINDING ARC SWEPT through the dark." She says it out loud, with great satisfaction. Describe ordinary things with new words, in new ways. She pivots again, flashlight in hand. Hmm …blinding seems a bit …overdone, perhaps?

"The round arc swept through the dark." Weak.

"The arc swept through the dark." Weaker still. She examines the flashlight. It gleams hopefully up at her, a dime-sized glow.

"The delicate round arc swept through the dark." Sweeping is a touch grandiose.

"The delicate round arc pushed ineffectually at the night." Hmm. Accurate, but not evocative.

"The delicate round arc …" - it isn't an arc.

"The delicate pinpoint of light danced in the dark." That's no way to start a bold tale of adventure. She sighs. It is accurate, though, and a good enough sentence, all in all. She shakes her head. Surely she can make this more powerful, more pregnant with menace. She rights a lawn chair and sinks into it, closing her eyes. Camping. She can be camping and hear a noise in the night.

"The sword of light pierced the darkness, a shaft of clarity cleaving the dangerous night." She snorts. The Sword of Light wielded by Acknar the All-Wise in the Time of the Great UnWeaving. She's not writing fantasy. She's not writing anything, except her name in the sky, with a feebly flickering flashlight.

"She groped for the flashlight in the numbing blackness, a sudden stab of light bisecting the night." Groping, numbing, stabbing, bisecting. Doctor Donna Does Danger. Maybe someone else is holding the light?

"She snapped awake, shocked into silence at the sudden sweep of brightness on the tent." No, she doesn't want to be the victim, she wants to be the intrepid explorer. She gazes sightlessly into the stars

She suddenly leaps to her feet, dashing into the shed and out again, kicking on the back door, arms full.

"Christopher!! Come out here!" She fumbles with the matches.

His sleep-blurred face is indulgently curious.

"Here, take this, walk to the garbage cans and back!"

He wanders amiably away, and she flushes with satisfaction at the swinging lantern, as a round blinding arc sweeps through the dark.

# My Father Was Ready

*Have I not been ready always at the iron door,*
*Not knowing to what country it opens—to death, or to more life*
*Am I not among the early risers?*
*- Mary Oliver*

He was ready, although he may have waved
you away several mornings, bent over
the dining room table piled high with bills,
policies; as he sorted through insurance papers,
placed copies of the will
in the great oak file cabinet behind the glass door.
Stubs of his fingers slowed his task, no feeling
left and forming the letters was a painful patience.
Through the dying grasses he laboured, bowed,
twisted as the crabapple limbs fruiting only death,
each evening to return to his place at the iron door.
That done, his mind prepared for more, if all to add
was a written journey, a tale-teller's tome
to place in a loved one's hand, embrace.

One never knows which direction that door will open,
though the signs, like cries of wild geese over moon-
hushed fields, remind of shortening light, of a wind
brooding round darkened house at night, of wingbeats
of the heart drifting, fading, in one last wave familiar,
before he walked out into that still night.

In the end, he was ready. Did he leave with no regrets?
That will wait for another time to tell
but when she opened up the metal box,
sitting in an office at the bank, she found all
where he left it, ready.

*Judith Frost*

# A Decent Burial

*Exodus 2, 3*

Don't bury your Egyptian in the sand
When the wind blows,
the bones will show.
Someone is watching from the margins
of the page.
He suddenly shows up in verse two
and the jig is up. You're off in the desert
for forty years of wasted time. Or is it?

Don't bury your Egyptian in the sand.
Take the body to the morgue and see
to a proper burial.
In the meantime, don't despair.
That wilderness is not as deserted
as you might think.
And the bush covered in creeper
may suddenly burst into flame.

Take off your sandals. Fall on your knees.
In the distance a pillar of fire blazes
to show the way into your night.

*Judith Frost*

# Father, Forgive Them

I am the traitor who traded you for a better deal.
I am the friends who scattered, leaving you to face the music alone.
I am the soldier who drove in the nails, just doing my job.
I am Pilate, washing my hands of responsibility.
I am the crowd, shouting catcalls, entertained by violent death.
I am the thief, sneering with my last breath.

You are the one petitioning God for my pardon.

*Marianne Jones*

# Spring Cleaning

Clean my house, Lord.
Come into my closets and start pitching:
that old, out-of-date fear,
that family heirloom resentment passed through generations,
that worry that seemed like such a good purchase when I
bought it,
that trunk I don't even want to open – pitch it, Lord.
Sweep away the cobwebs of false pride and selfish ambitions.
Leave nothing untouched.
Throw open the windows and let the Spirit-Breeze sweeten
the stale air.
Pour your sunlight into the dark corners where depression
broods.
Then don't let me take anything back, saying,
"But I might need this someday."

*Marianne Jones*

# Christmas Eve in Montreal

Dr. Gerald Hankins

ON CHRISTMAS EVE AROUND 5:00 p.m. I was walking along Boulevard Rene Levesque on my way to Candlelight Service at Notre Dame Cathedral. Maybe I should have felt something of the magic of Christmas Eve but around me there was little of warmth or good cheer. The ashen sky of a Montreal winter smothered the great city with a mantle of sombre greyness. Falling snowflakes might have dispelled some of the gloom but I saw none. There was no beauty or wonder in the gaudy parade of cars splashing through the slush. Shadowy strangers behind the wheel seemed remote and almost inhuman.

Crowds on the sidewalks bustled along, immersed in their own little affairs. Last minute shoppers dressed in warm winter coats lugged bags and boxes. Stopping to browse in front of one shop window, I was just beginning to delight in the warm display when a sharp jab in the ribs sent me sprawling in the murky snow. I got up quickly and brushed myself off. The man who had barged into me ran on without a word, pursued by his pals.

At the corner of Metcalfe Street, shoppers and strollers carefully circumvented a tall, rosy-cheeked Salvation Army man cheerfully ringing his bells. I noticed only a few coins at the bottom of his plastic kettle. Where was the Christmas spirit,

I asked myself. Did anyone care about anyone else? Were the people of Montreal as hard-hearted as Ebenezer Scrooge?

A brightly-lit flower shop with the sign "Jacques Beaudoin, Florist" looked like a haven away from the jostling crowd. I wandered in and joined the queue in front of the counter. The proprietor, a middle-aged man with thick gray hair, was doing his best to wrap up carnations, poinsettias and Christmas cactuses for the well-dressed shoppers.

Then the door opened and a boy of seven or eight appeared. His flimsy clothes were ragged and thread-bare and his running shoes ripped. A stained blue winter toque partly covered a mop of wild-looking hair. Without any hesitation he headed straight for the shop-keeper and asked, "Do you have any roses for my mother for ten cents?

M. Beaudoin paused for an instant, pursing his lips. "Just wait a moment and I'll see what we can do for you," he said. I thought I could spot the faintest trace of a smile.

A strange silence fell over the flower shop. M. Beaudoin served the other customers, one by one. They paid for their flowers and plants and then stood back. No one left the shop.

Finally the proprietor turned back to the boy and, nodding his head, announced, "I have good news for you. On Christmas Eve we have a special on roses for young fellows who want them for their mothers."

Taking the lad's dime, he carefully wrapped up a dozen long-stemmed roses and placed them in his arms. With a big smile on his face, the boy left the flower shop. The door closed quietly behind him.

# *The Gift of Imagination*

J. Paul Cooper

YOU'VE PROBABLY DONE IT HUNdreds of times and never gave it a second thought. Leaving the cinema, you turn to a friend and say, "Wouldn't it be great if….," and in a couple of sentences you tell your friend what you think is a great movie concept. What you've actually done is create a logline, the basis for a movie pitch. That story concept, succinctly expressed, is what puts into motion film projects that cost tens of millions of dollars to produce, employ hundreds of people in the film industry, launch the careers of actors and actresses and influence the thoughts, for better or worse, of people around the globe. That is the power of imagination.

Imagination is the precious gift that allows us to create. You won't write a literary masterpiece until you have imagined at least a part of the story in your mind. Construction can't begin on a new children's hospital until architects and engineers have imagined the end result and drawn the blueprints for the project.

Although we can take pride in many of our accomplishments, no one can really claim that his or her idea was completely original. The Wright brothers did create the first motor powered aircraft, but birds were using the basics or aerodynamics long before their aircraft left the ground. Everything we imagine is in some way influenced by the world we see around us, so only the Creator of our world can be described as truly original.

The earliest reference to our world is found in the Bible in the very first chapter of Genesis; it is described as "formless and empty." (Gen 1:2 NIV) God set to work, creating mountains and valleys, rivers and oceans, plants and animals, and Adam and Eve. So, did God imagine our world and then create it? Since the word "imagine" isn't used, it may be impossible to prove that He imagined the world first, but perhaps the answer lies in our genes. The Lord gave us the ability to make moral choices, to be aware of the eternal, and the desire to communicate and be heard by others. Perhaps the natural process of imagining and then creating is also one of the attributes He gave his children.

Although imagination is a gift from God and can be used for many good purposes, it also has the power to destroy. It's hard to conceive that millions of human beings could be slaughtered because of one man's imagination, but just the mention of the name Hitler reminds us of the devastation that one man's thoughts can cause. Even in Heaven, where one would never expect evil thoughts to emerge, Lucifer imagined himself rising above God and he was banished from the City, along with one-third of the angels. Now he exits in a state of perpetual desperation, imagining what eternity in Hell will be like.

Is there any limit to the power of imagination? Yes, but only if God intervenes. In the account of the Tower of Babel, God, referring to the fact that the people of the time spoke the same language, stated, "Nothing they plan to do will be impossible for them." (Gen 11:6 NIV) God acted immediately, introducing various languages, so that there was a limit placed on the ability of humans to communicate with each other. Today email, cell phones, internet social networks and the rise of English as an international language is bringing humanity back to where it was at the time of the Tower of Babel. Once again, it seems that anything is possible.

In a very real sense, our ability to imagine and create makes our need for God's intervention and protection even greater. The same men and women who work in science labs to create new medications can also create biological weapons. The same men who design websites to help us communicate with family members around the globe can also design pornography sites that destroy lives for a profit.

It's a very sobering thought for those who express their imaginations through the art of writing; whether it be poetry, novels, essays or screenplays. Imagination. A gift from God. A powerful tool. A great responsibility.

# Angels About Me

Irene Bastian

I GRABBED MY HEAVY LINED JEAN jacket, stepped into the garage and slipped on my rubber boots. The old dog looked up at me as if to say "Do I really have to go with you? It's miserable outside."

I bent over and gave her a pat. "Okay old girl, I'll let you off this time." I headed to the corrals. Walking was awkward as the earlier mud impressions from my boots were filling with snow and starting to freeze. I shook my head in disbelief. This was May.

Red, an older cow my husband and I had bought a few years prior, was earlier showing signs of calving. We didn't have a proper birthing pen, but used a smaller building as a shelter where a birthing mother could get in out of the weather. Our small herd was gentle and easy to handle, except for Red. No matter what we did for her, she never became friendly.

Approaching the corral, I noticed Red wasn't outside. I rattled the chain on the gate and called out so that I wouldn't startle her. I reached the doorway of the building and kept talking while my eyes adjusted to the dim light inside. "How are you doing?" I asked, my eyes focusing on her form near the back of the shelter.

"Oh," I exclaimed," You've had it already. Is everything alright?" I leaned my body over to the right to get a better look at the calf. I didn't step in any closer, as I wasn't about to get trapped in the building with a new mother. As I shifted my body, my eye caught a swift movement from Red and then wham! I felt myself being driven into the doorframe. When my feet hit the ground again, I spun around to get away. Whack! I was hit from behind and went flying through the air, arms flailing. One arm caught my new glasses and they flew off my face. Frantically I tried to grab them as I descended towards the ground. I missed and landed with the glasses somewhere under my chest.

Slowly I raised myself up on my hands and knees. Bang! I was knocked flat again. I was shocked because I figured since I wasn't near her newborn, Red would leave me alone. Not so; she was enraged! Each time I tried to get up, she hit me from behind. I found myself becoming a human plow as I was pushed around the corral making a trail through the snow, mud and manure. Finally I became trapped between the building and the water trough.

Red stood on my back with one front foot and pawed at me with the other. I became a human trampoline. I threw a gloved hand over my neck to protect it. If I moved or raised my head, Red slammed it with hers. "Stop it, please stop it! Help!" I cried. I wished the dog had come with me. She might have been able to distract the cow long enough for me to get up. I thought of my family. Would they find me here trampled to death when they got home? I could feel Red's hot breath on the back of my head and hear her irate grunts as she fought to destroy me. "What a way to die," I thought, "face down in the manure!"

Suddenly I bolted my head up realizing I hadn't called on the only one who could help me. "Lord, help me!" I called. Once again I felt my face dig into the muck with another hit from behind.

Then, abruptly, Red stopped, turned, and ran to the far side of the corral. I raised my head and stared at her. Her flaming eyes focused not on me, but on something above me.

I followed her gaze. I didn't see anything, but she certainly did. Slowly I got up keeping one eye pinned on the cow, while trying to see what it was that she was staring at. Motionless, she seemed hypnotized, focusing on a spot above me. I took a couple of steps. She remained rigid. Her glazed eyes were frightful. Would she let me out I wondered? I headed over to the railed fence. Red never budged; her eyes glanced briefly as I moved but then remained fixed on something just above me. I felt someone unseen on each side of me, giving me physical support and coaxing me along. I vaguely remember reaching the fence, but somehow I was on the other side of it. Doubled over and holding my sides, I turned towards the house, then stopped and eyed the haystack. Maybe I should rest a bit first. Something, or someone, urged me to keep going. I trudged towards the house leaning on my helpers for support. I knew instinctively that God had sent his angels to minister to me. I was not afraid.

As I stepped into the house, the angels released me. I stumbled into the kitchen and reached for the phone. I felt pain sear across my ribs and chest. My breathing was rapid and labored. How much internal damage would there be?

At the hospital, staff and onlookers stared at my dung-saturated clothing. "I had a fight with a cow and the cow won," I told the nurse.

Once examined by the doctor I was whisked to the x-ray department. After completing the x-rays, the technician spoke, "I'll be right back." Upon returning he uttered, "Okay we get to go for another ride." An ultra sound was the next agenda item. "Your doctor will be right with you," he stated as he returned me to my emergency room. I knew from his aloofness that something was wrong.

The doctor entered. I had three broken ribs and perhaps a few cracked ones. The sternum was intact, but I was quite bruised front and back and had cuts and scrapes on the back of my neck where the cow's hooves had pawed me but no spinal damage showed. Had I not shifted my body just before the cow hit me, a direct blow on the sternum could have been fatal. My heavy jacket and the soft wet ground had probably saved me from more serious damage. "While everything appears to be okay internally, we are concerned about possible damage, particularly the spleen. We'll keep you overnight for observation. If the spleen is damaged we may have to do emergency surgery," the doctor stated.

I prayed there was no serious damage. I didn't have time for surgery. It was spring seeding time. Doctors and nurses kept checking on me as the night wore on. Over and over the attack played in my mind. Had I imagined divine intervention? No, the fear in Red's eyes as she stared at that apparition was as real as my pain. No, I wouldn't have made it out of there and back to the house unaided. Angels had surrounded me. I had felt their touch. Everything was going to be okay.

In the morning my hubby arrived with my weirdly bent glasses, news that the calf was fine and that many prayers were sent on my behalf. I was cleared for discharge with a warning to take it easy while the ribs healed.

It took time for the ribs and bruising to heal. It took more time for me to have the courage to walk among the herd again, but a summer filled with the tasty hamburgers courtesy of Red aided the healing process.

As people heard of my ordeal, I learned that angry cattle never give up until they have killed their victims or are distracted. Often farmers are killed in attacks because there is no escape and no one to intervene. Praise God for divine intervention! Thank God for placing his angels about me. "Are not all angels ministering spirits, sent to serve those who will inherit salvation?" (Hebrews 1:14 NIV)

# The Gift

Isabel Didriksen

ON A COLD, WINTRY DAY IN February, I received a phone call from my friend, asking if I could use a fur coat.

"It's not real fur, but you go to church and you could wear it there."

A few weeks went by and it became evident winter was not going away. I decided one Saturday morning to make a visit. After a little "catching up" on the news in her world, she took me into the bedroom and showed me a three-quarter length coat with long white fur accented by black and grey stripes. It was beautiful!

"Try it on."

I slipped my arms into the sleeves and instantly felt a cozy warmth as I drew it around me.

"Oh, it fits you just perfectly," she exclaimed with a big smile. "Turn around. Look, it's just right."

"Are you sure you want to give this away? Is it okay with your husband?"

"Oh yeah. He gave it to me for Christmas a few years ago, but it doesn't fit anymore. No one in my family will ever use it. Take it and wear it to church," she said happily.

After more visiting and a cup of tea, I departed with my new treasure. As it happened, the weather turned extremely cold, so several times in the following weeks, I decided to wear the coat—even if it wasn't to church. I was going to be warm! I deeply appreciated the gift because it was comforting to snuggle in when the temperature hovered around minus 30.

But what if I had left it hanging in the closet? When the thermometer dipped low, I could say, "Just think, my friend gave me that beautiful coat, isn't it lovely? But I don't deserve it, or maybe she didn't really mean for me to use it." So I left it hanging there.

That warm coat reminds me of God's love. He offers love to me, telling me to "put on" His love, to feel it around me, to snuggle into it. He offers it freely, but I get caught up in doubts and fears and leave His love "hanging in the closet." The chills of trials and heartaches come, but I keep trying to get along without "using" God's love.

"I'm doing okay. It would be nice to feel God's love around me, but I'll wait. For now, I'll do things 'my way.'"

If I'd never worn the coat, or left it for only very special occasions, my friend would have been offended. She wanted me to use it when the weather was cold.

Similarly, God doesn't want me to wait until I have a "special" need or occasion to accept His love. He wants me to take it and use it and feel it around me now. But He won't force me to do that; He has given me a free will. I must choose to gratefully accept His love, to realize how great a price He paid for that love and how sad He is to see me refusing to accept it.

No, I don't deserve God's love but He has given it freely to me. All I have to do is take it, wrap it around me and snuggle in.

# Anger – A landmine of Satan

Jan Cox

*"In a controversy, the instant we feel anger, we have already ceased striving for truth and have begun striving for ourselves,"*
*~ theologian Abraham J. Heschel*

As I slammed the door, the noise reverberated around the house. Then, silence. I ran to the bed, threw myself across it and pounded my fists into the mattress.

*How dare he? Why didn't he want to listen to me?*

I cried out in a loud voice, "I hate you!"

The lump in my throat grew and tears trickled down my cheek. Gasping for breath, I shuddered. My chest burned as I clenched my fist. A low sob erupted from deep within me. I tried to draw another breath but a cry escaped my lips and more tears fell. I buried my head in my arms as my whole body dissolved in anguish.

That was seven years ago. I can't recall the reason for the breakdown but I still feel the emotions. This wasn't a one time occurrence. Time and again I would find myself upset, often slamming doors. It was fortunate that my husband was handy and could fix those hinges!

Anger is one of Satan's landmines – one way to distract us

from godly living.

In James 4:1 (NIV), James asks, "What causes fights and quarrels among you?"

When I look back at who I was then and how I have changed, I see that Jesus really can transform us. I was totally into myself. Everything revolved around my feelings, my opinions and my solutions.

James continues, "Don't they (quarrels) come from your desires that battle within you? You want something but don't get it." (James 4:1, 2 NIV)

What he says is so true. My anger had stemmed from not getting my own way. I have a deep desire to control. The difference in the new me is how I relate to people. Since finding the love of Jesus, I have wanted to learn how to be like Him. There was no quick solution. It was and continues to be hard work.

I had to learn to sit and be still and listen to God. It was an effort. The first attempt lasted no more than five minutes. But gradually by repeating the exercise every day, I extended my time. As I did this He showed me that this life wasn't all about me.

James says, "Submit yourselves, then, to God. Resist the devil, and he will flee from you. Come near to God and he will come near to you." (James 4:7 NIV)

Letting God speak to me revealed that my husband wasn't the problem – I was. My hubby never raised his voice when I got angry. He is very gentle and kind. We clashed only when I wanted things done my way and my way only. I asked God for help and He has shown me that I can always count on Him to help me see things through His eyes.

My capacity for anger is still there. It is how I deal with the anger that matters. Every day has challenges and the possibility of plans to be interrupted and feelings hurt. Only God can help me maneuver over the land mines safely without hurting myself or others. I pray each day for God to guide me, to help me learn to live in love and peace with everyone.

# *Beyond Reason*

Eunice Matchett

THE MAN PRESSED HIS CHIN against his chest, letting his hood take the brunt of the storm, and forced his numbed legs forward. Pain accompanying freezing flesh stabbed his fingers. He curled them into his palms, letting the ends of his mitts hang loose. Still the cold found them. He clenched his fists tighter, wondering what had possessed him to come out on such a day. Lifting his head, he looked down the trail to see how far he'd come, but it was too late. Evening shadows, long since grown old, gave way to darkness. An icy wind sucked the falling snow into itself, then hurled it at him. His head dropped, and he hunched his shoulders against the freezing weapon, stumbling on, determined to reach home before night.

His back ached from the heavy pack, and he stopped to move it, then pushed one trembling leg forward. Its foot sank through the snow, touching ground. He lifted the other, moved it beyond the first. Pain shot up past his knee and he bent down, rubbed it, then lifted his head to get his bearings.

Wind assaulted him, biting his cheeks, stinging his eyes. He stumbled backwards, arms flailing. The pack slipped to one side, and he crashed into the snow. A two-foot white wall surrounded him and small, icy snowflakes poured from the sky. He thought of his bed with its thick, down-filled duvet, and rolled onto his hands and knees, crawling to the obstacle he'd hit. Protruding roots dug into his knees and brittle willow branches snapped under his weight. That could only mean one thing. He caught his breath and cold fear washed over him. He had wandered off the trail. His hands attacked the snow, pawing, sending it in a flurry behind him. A log appeared. Then another, until he'd exposed a section of a partially built cabin wall. He thought of his own, and his stomach growled, demanding food.

He grasped the top log, pulling himself to his feet, but his world swirled around him, the ground came up, and he crumpled back down. He needed a few minutes rest. That was all. His hunger must have fed on his strength.

Curling up in the hole he'd dug, he pushed his back against logs and folded an arm over his face. That'd drive the wind crazy if it had a mind to get at him. But he'd only rest a few minutes, then continue. After all, he must be close to home. His eyes drifted closed.

He woke with a start, and glanced around. The storm had abated. A bright moon shone between spindly tree branches. Off in the distance, something called, shrill and haunting. It came again. A wolf, howling into the soundless night. He shivered. It was time to leave. He pushed himself into a sitting position, but his arm trembled from the effort and he fell back down, still too tired. Besides, they were miles away. And even if they weren't, why should he fear? In the wilderness, he was the man, the superior being, the god-animal.

He sank back into his hollow. The howl came again, closer. Seconds later, an answer sounded, then an answer to the answer. Silent steps sent warning vibrations through the snow as the wolves slunk closer. And closer. He raised his head. They were all around him, resting on their haunches. Their tongues lolled over gleaming teeth and plumes of steam rose from their open mouths. More wolves skulked from behind, coming nearer, their bodies trembling with anticipation. The man felt their breath, smelled their hunger and it matched his own.

A green streak stretched across the clear, star-filled sky. It shifted, widening. A brilliant strip much the same as a single streak of forked lightning, only green, highlighted one side and a shadow of the brightness spread out from the vibrant backbone. The whole spectacle swayed to silent music, its shape altering from bright to dull. Then the highest point swirled downward, into a semicircle, forming a wolf's head, its eyes yearning, pleading.

It tore the man to his core, moving him to respond. But what did he have, that he could give a wolf?

The eerie light's shape changed, obliterating the wolf head, and its top swayed like arms of a belly dancer. Its bottom contracted, twirling, spinning, and dropped to a point. The man watched, too afraid to scream, too terrified to run.

The pointed mass rested above him, its end turning up like a crooked finger beckoning him, drawing him into itself. He rose from the ground, hovering above the wolves. Then he felt warm again. His hunger pains relieved.

Like a young man again, experiencing an arctic winter for the first time, he headed east. His cabin was east, was it not? But if it wasn't, what did it matter? He was warm and nourished.

Tree trunks scraped against his side, but he felt no pain. Snow-heavy bows swooshed over his head, dropping clumps of snow, blurring his vision. He shook it away, and followed no path, feeling safer away from the god-animal's trails. The shifting winter lights intensified, lighting his way, but producing no shadows. He pressed on, needing to find shelter, a place to sleep and digest his meal.

The ground climbed, tiring him, then fell away. He paused, looking down a bank at the frozen river, and remembered a trail leading to it, and a cave along its edge. It wasn't far. He gave the river one more glance but he saw it at many different spots all at the same time. Disturbed, he wondered where he'd left his mind. Then he moved without choosing to do so. His snowshoes seemed weightless and the rhythm in which he walked felt alien. Where were his legs? He couldn't find them, yet he moved. It puzzled him, but he felt no fear. Maybe he was more tired than he thought. Yes, that was it. He moved faster. His cabin must be close, his bed waiting.

He took a deep breath and hot humid air, smelling of blood, filled his lungs. His fear returned, and he looked around, but black surrounded him. He must be in his sleigh. That had to be it. The sleigh turned, and he pulled the blanket off his face. This time he could see. Wolves, big, gray, hungry looking wolves approached. A growl vibrated around him. He stepped backwards but there was nowhere to go. The black returned and the wolves disappeared. His air thinned, making him breathe twice as fast for half as much air. He kept on fighting, but the black got blacker. His eyes closed, giving in to mounting fatigue.

Then he awoke. The northern lights swayed in a smooth, hypnotic fashion, pulling him towards them, engulfing him. He looked down at a pack of wolves, resting on their stomachs, front legs extended, and heads resting on them, sleeping, contented. A silver cord rose from each wolf, the thickest coming from the biggest wolf he'd ever laid eyes upon. The cords joined, forming a large one that drifted upwards, toward him. He twisted around for a better view. *Oh no!* It clung to him. His fright echoed all around, growing louder. He grabbed the cord and yanked with all his strength but it refused to loosen its hold.

The wolves rose to their haunches, pointed their noses at him and howled, pulling him back. He fought them. Up here, he was free, warm and not hungry. They howled louder, tugging harder, gaining ground until his strength gave out and he floated down, still free, yet a prisoner.

*

Spring came early to the north and with it, better prospects of food. The old gray wolf lumbered away from the abandoned cabin he'd stayed near all winter, except to hunt. A trail crossed his path and a familiar scent rose from the packed ground. He followed the scent to a human's den. Its entrance stood open, and he stepped inside, cautious, ready to dash at the first whiff of danger. His gaze swept the room and he smelled the air. It reeked of human, yet he felt no aversion. Braver, he walked around, smelling the floor, listening, still ready to bolt. He came to a bed in the furthest recess of the den. His head jerked up and he looked around. How did he know it was a bed? He sniffed up one of its legs, across its side. Duck feathers! How could there be duck feathers without bones and meat? He backed away, still smelling, listening. The floor creaked but otherwise all remained still. His apprehension quieted, he returned to the bed, staked it out as his territory, and jumped on top. It felt soft, and the wolf curled up, pushing his nose under his back leg. He closed his eyes, content, as if he'd come home.

# Tableland

I could celebrate Communion
at this tableland
whose golden altar cloth is laid
beneath the elements of harvest.
No matter that the cloth
trails, gully-pleated,
sodden-edged
through some forgotten little creek;
I too, am soiled with things of earth
as I approach the altar rail.
But here,
under cathedral skies
where light is pale and pure,
God comes to me
with cleansing,
sustenance
and peace.

*Sophie Stark*

# Hillsides

Logged-over areas:
skinned knuckles
on the clenched fists
of foothills;
raw and tender,
healing slowly,
so slowly,
under pale green skin.

*Sophie Stark*

# Highway #1

High overcast
eeries the sunlight;
changes colours
until spring grass,
no longer green,
but threaded through
with last year's growth,
becomes a silver tweed.

*Sophie Stark*

# Callings

I am glad to be a servant
in the household of my Lord,
but my service must be faithful and complete;
for I owe to Him allegiance
which is arduous, but sweet.
It requires the best my talents can afford.

I am one of many players
in the orchestra of God,
and my part is neither intricate nor long;
it's just a melody of praises
that repeats itself in song,
while it carries all my love for Him abroad.

I am called a story teller
by the children of my King,
so for them I write the saga of a Friend;
One who shares their life's adventure
from beginning to its end;
who in wisdom, will provide for everything.

So I find a deep contentment
in the work of every day;
each achievement is a tribute to His grace.
And the one reward I covet when I see my Master's face:
"You have been a faithful servant," He will say.

*Sophie Stark*

# Strangers in a Crowd

I am not you, you are not me,
Strangers, a crowd, we stop to speak.
My private memories, loves and fears,
Are not yours, and yet it's clear,
I have a need and if I share,
A portion of me,
Perhaps you'll care.

I know not what you dream,
You view,
Nor what you see,
Feel and do,
Unmasked,
The shadows flow to and fro,
We interweave,
Elude and gently sow,
The fabric of friendship,
Softly spun
With spoken thoughts
On careful tongues.

You can know me and I know you,
A rare and tender caring too,
And nourished
It might bloom and grow,
Life's aim, life's wish,
We may know.

*Cynthia Post*

# My Soul's Retreat

Feathers of silver mist waft upward,
Trees, clouds mirrored below.
Water gently rippling, lapping,
Sparkling sunlight warms my soul.

The loon's lonely, haunting cry,
The grebe's harsh, raspy call.
Soaring osprey, swooping, searching
Bid a welcome to my soul.

Whistling wind through the needles,
Churning water strikes the shore.
Dark clouds, rain swirling, pelting
… nature's forces ignite my soul.

Mountains, clouds, purple etchings,
Pink skies, water calm and still.
Forest green and gold reflecting.
Peace returns to my soul.

*Cynthia Post*

# The Carousel

Geraldine Nicholas

SEVEN-YEAR OLD MARIA AND five-year old Peter presented me with a birthday gift wrapped in Disney paper. "We used our piggy-bank money to buy this for you, Grandma," Peter told me. Inside was a musical carousel with two children riding on the back of a white swan. When I turned the key on its base the swan twirled in circles to the tune, "It's A Small World."

"This is beautiful!" I exclaimed. I wound it up and the three of us danced around the room to the cheerful tune. This became a ritual whenever they visited our home.

One day during one of their visits Peter and the carousel disappeared after lunch.

"Where are you Peter?" I called out to him.

Maria's eyes lit up. "I think he's playing "hide and seek!"

We searched under beds, behind couches and doors. Finally we found him sitting cross-legged in the corner of a closet. He was weeping. The swan's head was in his hand.

"I broke it, Grandma," he muttered tearfully.

"Mama told you it wasn't a toy, Peter," Maria scolded. "You weren't supposed to play with it!"

"I wasn't playing with it," he insisted. "I was only winding it up."

"Well you weren't supposed to wind it up. That was

Grandma's job," she reminded him.

"I forgot," he replied sadly.

Maria and I sat down in front of the closet and Peter crawled into my lap.

"Sorry, Grandma." he whispered.

I kissed away his tears. "Accidents happen. Grandpa can probably fix it with crazy glue."

"You promise you're not mad at me?" He had to be sure.

"I promise," I nodded.

Maria wasn't so quick to promise. "Peter…that carousel cost us a lot of money!" she declared indignantly.

His face screwed into grief again. Soon tears were streaming down Maria's face. We all huddled on the floor in a comforting bear hug for awhile.

An hour later the two of them were playing a board game and chattering happily about their anticipated trip to a wave pool the next day. Maria had already forgotten her grievance with her brother and was content to leave the fate of the carousel to her Grandpa and his crazy glue magic. And Peter, convinced he was forgiven, could get on with enjoying the rest of his day.

No wonder Jesus values childlikeness so highly in our relationship with Him! He proclaimed, "I tell you the truth, unless you change and become like little children, you will never enter the kingdom of heaven." (Matthew 18:3b – NIV ) While not all childlike traits are endearing, there are obviously some that He never wants His children to outgrow. Things like genuine regret when we have done wrong; truthfulness; transparency; and an eager desire for forgiveness and reconciliation so we can abandon grudges quickly and get on with living a vibrant, joyful life.

Grandpa never could repair the broken carousel. It remains an endearing reminder of the valuable lesson my grandchildren taught me that day. For I, even more than they, have no time to waste…and must get on with living life to the full.

# I Can't Find Him

Ella Sailor

HER YEARS WERE MANY–SOME suggested a hundred–but Granny would simply grin and shake her head; her tribe, the Loucheux, didn't keep records way back then.

We met through a mutual friend on a frigid Arctic night, and Granny presumed on a friendship at once. I dropped in on her often over the long winter months and found her to be a gracious and generous friend. She was a woman of faith and sought to win her neighbors along with her own family.

On occasion, a great-grandchild came knocking,, "Granny says you haven't b'en." Or like the morning she summoned me, "Granny needs you to go to the lighthouse." I hurried to comply. My short time in Dawson City hadn't allowed time to acquaint myself with its many historical attractions.A lighthouse, I pondered as I struggled with long-johns and heavy sweats, topping them with down-filled parka and Yukon boots–where could it be? And what could an elderly lady possibly want from a lighthouse?

The diminutive and slightly bent figure met me at the door. Handing me an invoice and cash, she instructed,"Take him to the lighthouse." I chuckled as I headed off to pay her light bill.

Summer arrived and with it abundance of vegetation. Often we spent the day roaming the hills gathering wild rhubarb, Indian tea, and edible mushrooms. Try as we would, the delectable birch mushroom eluded us. Up Midnight Dome, down the valleys, and across the Yukon River the stands of birch yielded no such delicacy in their shade. Her disappointment was palpable; she would shake her head as we headed home, "I can't find him."

We were from two different worlds, Granny and I. It was never more obvious than in our manner of communication. She could sit for long periods without saying a word–I could scarce keep quiet. At times she seemed to forget I was still there. After one such lengthy conversational hiatus, she commented, "This morning I pick the Foxtail."

Since she had earlier discussed the healing benefits of Indian Tea, I was fascinated. Could there really be a redeeming quality to Foxtail? I leaned forward eagerly expecting her to go on. Granny sipped her tea, rocked slowly, nibbled her cookie . . . rocked some more. Thinking she had lost her train of thought, I ventured, "What did you do with the Foxtail, Granny?"

The look on her face scarce needed interpretation. "I put him in the garbage," she muttered, "he gets stuck in my socks." Clearly she thought I was daft.

But I was always captivated by her tales of the early days. Her stories were spellbinding, like the time her tribe was destitute–starvation imminent. Even then Granny had a relationship with her Creator. She felt Him directing her to take the firearm and go into the forest. She described her adventure, "I see the big moose there; I shoot him. I go back and tell the men, 'I shoot him; you get him.' "

During a particularly virulent case of salmonella, Granny spent many weeks in a coma. She recalled that during this time she found herself crossing the frozen Yukon River. A teenager joined her and they walked on together. Open water lay before them; undeterred the lad continued, but Granny heard a voice,"It is not your time. You must go back." She watched the lonely figure go on alone…walking on the water. Many days later she woke and knew he would not be back. He had crossed the river–he had taken his own life.

Granny's tiny frame was becoming more feeble with age. I increased my visits. She was now unable to walk or care for herself. Each time I found her sitting in the same place on her little couch. Her frailty left her speech barely audible. Each time I called those responsible for her care she would be bathed, and again left on the couch. A week or two later the scenario was repeated.

It concerned me that her small moccasins were nearly obscured by the terrible swelling of her feet. They must see her terrible discomfort! They could at least wash her feet.

My thundering thoughts were interrupted by a still small voice, "Why don't you wash her feet?"

I was taken aback. Where did that come from? Just a stray thought.

"Wash her feet," the voice persisted.

There's no wash basin.

"You have one at home."

It's more than two blocks in the frigid cold.

"It will soon be dark."

Granny would be embarrassed if I asked to wash her feet.

"Ask her and see."

I dared to broach the subject and the dear saint nodded so enthusiastically I was ashamed of my reluctance. Slipping and stumbling my way home over the frozen ruts, my thoughts centered on Jesus; I knew what He would do; I also knew I was not in His league.

As I worked the moccasins from her swollen feet a shower of dry skin littered the floor. Her toe nails were broken and crumbling. How could anyone leave her like this?

And so it began–washing and massaging her feet, returning every few days to repeat the process. Tears filled her leathery wrinkles and escaped down her cheeks as she repeated her little story in a half whisper:

"When I am young–always I care for the elders in my tribe. Now I am old; the Lord He send me you," she would pause, nodding her head, wiping tears, and sometimes patting my hand; "when you are old, He send someone. He care for you, too."

In God's perfect time, He gave Granny the desire of her heart–she crossed the river. I rejoiced in tears. I look forward to our heavenly reunion. I see her tending her small fire, I smell the aroma of birch mushrooms sizzling in the giant pan. Her eyes sparkling, she will smile at me and nod, "I find him."

# A Message for These Times

Martha Anderson

IN A TINY, WAR-THREATENED country bordering on the eastern shores of the Mediterranean Sea 2600 years ago lived a relatively-unknown man. Of his genealogy, family, or occupation we have no record. We know nothing about the man; nothing except one short, simple pronouncement carrying his byline: Habakkuk.

The Babylonian armies are advancing westward and are about to trample the Judean country and its inhabitants in their path. With questions and misgivings, Habakkuk begins his brief forewarning of pending judgment. Why should God's people be punished by a nation worse than theirs, he wonders. Yet he waits on God to answer the perplexities of his heart. In words that have remained a challenge over the years, the Lord answers him.

"Write the vision and make it plain on tablets, that he may run who reads it" (Habakkuk 2:2a NKJV).

God made him to understand the message was not for him alone, but to the nation. The writer's confidence grows as he pours out his heart to God in intercession for his homeland. Despite the pending doom Habakkuk catches a vision of a glorious future for all who trust God. In the face of imminent danger, he sounds out a message of hope. With renewed confidence, he writes, "Though the fig tree may not blossom, Nor fruit be on the vines; Though the labor of the olive may fail, And the fields yield no food; Though the flocks be cut off from the fold, And there be no herds in the stalls—Yet I will rejoice in the Lord, I will joy in the God of my salvation. The Lord God is my strength" (Habakkuk 3:17-19a NKJV).

Of all the priceless gems contained in the 56 verses of Habakkuk's prophecy, none has had more impact through the centuries than the brief sentence: "The righteous shall live by his faith."

I wonder, when the prophet Habakkuk scratched his God-given message in Hebrew symbols on a leather scroll in 600 B.C., did he even faintly envision that his words would have any significance beyond that particular time and location? As he saw his people continue to disobey God and suffer under the domination of the Babylonians, did he question whether his warning had been worthwhile?

Writing to his own generation regarding their immediate circumstances, I doubt that he could have envisioned the impact his words would have on future generations. He could not have known that years later the Holy Spirit would use those words to set on fire the heart of the Apostle Paul. Yet the words, "The just shall live by his faith" (Habakkuk 2:4b NKJV) became the beacon light for all Paul's preaching and writing. Three times he quoted these words, making them the theme of his letters.

Years later a newly-ordained priest, Martin Luther, read this quote in Romans 1:17, and realized for the first time that salvation was by faith alone. That led to his conversion and consequently to the reformation of the 16th century.

Two hundred years later a defeated and unhappy clergyman returned to London, England, from a preaching mission to the colonies in Georgia. Little did this 34-year-old Methodist missionary suspect what God had in store for him on May 24, 1738.

In his journal he wrote of that life-changing event. These are his words: "In the evening I went very unwillingly to a society in Aldersgate Street, where one was reading Luther's *Preface to the Epistle to the Romans.* About a quarter before nine, while the leader was describing the change which God works in the heart through faith in Christ, I felt my heart strangely warmed. I felt I did trust in Christ alone for salvation; and an assurance was given me that He had taken away my sins, even mine, and saved me from the law of sin and death." That day John Wesley's intellectual conviction was transformed into a personal experience.

The ministry of John Wesley, and his brother, Charles, in the following years, resulted in the conversion of literally thousands. So the ripples created by one single manuscript continues to spread in ever larger circles. Though the message comes from a man unknown, his words have influenced us all.

As in the time of Habakkuk, we can trust in God who is the One Constant in an unstable world. When all around we see moral decay and the consequences that follow, we, too, can trust the Unfailing One. We, too, can listen to God and write the message He lays on our hearts, making it plain on the printed page.

Through publication and even in personal letters, we can give out the message of a glorious future for the children of God. We can minister, not only to our generation, but to people yet unborn. Who knows how God will use our words in years to come? Any awards or recognition, any remuneration for our efforts, fade in comparison with the satisfaction of knowing that through our manuscripts, others can come to trust our Creator and Redeemer.

The Apostle Paul put it this way: "But what things were gain to me, these I have counted loss for Christ. But indeed I count all things loss for the excellence of the knowledge of Christ Jesus my Lord, for whom I have suffered the loss of all things, and count them as rubbish, that I may gain Christ" (Philippians 2:7,8 NKJV)

PRAYER: Dear Lord, may our goal ever be to make Your message clear, May we listen to Your voice and write out of the overflow of our hearts that readers will be encouraged to trust the God of our Salvation in these uncertain times. Amen.

# A Father's Love

Pam Mytroen

NOW WAS THE BEST TIME TO approach my father, Benito. He had taken his supper and was reclining behind our stone house.

"Father," I whispered.

He looked up. A smile lifted his wrinkled face.

My chest tightened. I didn't want to leave. He had been a good father, but I was sick of books, and sheep and pruning grape vines.

"Aurelio?" The willow rocker squeaked as he pushed his large frame from it. "Bring me the stylus. I'll check your lesson."

"I'm finished with words," I said, smacking a stone railing. "Spelling is a waste."

Laughter erupted from his chest, and a bubble of joy rose in my throat. My father's buoyant spirit always lightened the mood. But tonight I would not allow it to change my mind.

Father's rhythmic breathing drummed the night air. I would rather he guessed my plans than have to tell him myself.

"I've always wanted to see the ocean." Disgusted at the weakness in my voice, I cleared my throat. "I'm leaving at dawn."

He lowered his head and furrowed his brow until his eyes disappeared. "The ocean," he said, breathing deeply. "Waters test a man's endurance."

He had called me a man. Did this mean he trusted me? Would he really let me go? A shiver ran up my arms. My friend would be waiting in the valley the next morning. I must go regardless of how my father felt.

"I'll show you, Father. You'll see," I said jumping over the railing and landing with both feet solid on the ground. "I won't give up and run home."

Father lifted his arms and then dropped them heavily to his sides. "You'll always be welcome here, Son." He turned his head towards the sheep where they rested beside our stream.

"You mean you can always use my help." The bitterness in my voice surprised me. Night after night I would wrap my bleeding hands in olive-oil rags and vow to find a better life. Yet now, when I finally revealed my soul, it sounded too harsh. I wanted to run back to my father. Instead, I turned and started toward the stable.

The birds had fallen silent and the only song on the night was the whistle of grass as I walked. I wished my father would say something, anything. I had always bristled when he called me with another chore, but tonight my hands ached for the smooth wood of a shepherd's cane. *No,* I told myself. *I must not weaken. I've wanted to leave for too long.*

"You'll need your canteen," he said finally.

"It's packed."

"And a good steed," he added. "What about bread and cheese?"

I had already watered and fed my horse and taken the left-over roast and wine from the cellar after supper. "There will be plenty of olives along the way," was all I said as I neared the stable.

I stopped. The taste of honey-cakes filled my mouth as I remembered the harvest feasts we enjoyed around Father's table. *Keep going.* Never again did I want to awaken to the gong of the bell.

A tiny ping resounded from the bell. Even now, after I'd been abrupt with my father and announced my sudden plans, he still played our favourite game, tossing pebbles at the black iron bell, high up on the watch tower. Didn't he know how difficult he was making this? Would it hurt to throw another pebble, see if I could hit that bell one last time? Instead of playing along, though, I stood still, with my back towards him.

"I traveled to the ocean once," he said behind me. "It's a fitting place for you."

I turned then. "What do you mean?" I noticed he had rolled his right hand into a tight fist. I felt myself weaken. Was Father angry with me? He had always been gentle. Strict, and hard to reason with sometimes, but never cruel. Maybe this was too much for him, though, my hasty departure. I backed up a step.

Father put both hands behind his back and surveyed the ground in front of him, selecting an even spot where no rocks would throw him off balance. A cool breeze lifted the dust at his feet and clouded his face. Would he strike me?

"My brother is still here. He can prune the vines." I said, hoping to appease him.

"I have not looked forward to this day," said Father. "However, as you feel called to freedom, I must leave you with this." He leaned in.

"Let me be," I said backing towards the stable where my horse was already saddled.

"You're lost," he said, his voice thick and swollen. He advanced on me and grasped my wrist.

"I knew you would object," I said, straining to free myself.

He swung his fist out from behind his back and opened it. "A boy needs guidance," he said, revealing an object in his palm.

I gasped. "A compass?" I stared at my father. The soft grey eyes had clouded. I plucked the instrument from his large hand and traced my finger around its dial. "To take me through the mountains?" I glanced to the north. Already the evening sky shrouded the hills in darkness.

My father sighed. The pruning shears had blistered his hands and calluses grazed the back of my neck as he pulled me to his chest.

The scent of lanolin and earth circled me as I tucked my head under the warmth of his chin. He held me without saying a word. I wondered why I wanted to leave his side. For so long his eyes had shone with pride as I worked with him. I hesitated, then pushed myself away.

Father's voice was low, broken. "Yes, this compass will direct you away. To the shore." Before he looked to the heavens I noticed the glistening in his eyes. "But I hope you'll use it, someday," he said, "to find your way back home."

# Takin' Notice

Susan Roberts Plett

ZEB'S ON HIS WAY HOME FROM THE city, just him and a truckload of wood bombin' along dirt roads singin' and thinkin' about board feet, and if he's got enough 2x8s and where should he put the winda and BANG! he smacks a porcupine right off the road. He slows down a little but there ain't much he can do now. He turns the radio up and starts diggin' around on the floor, tryin' to find his Rona mug before there's coffee everywhere and he hears someone say "Watch the road."

Zeb jumps and looks up and out the winda but there ain't nothin' there. He frowns and looks beside him and there's a guy sittin' in the passenger seat, holdin' somethin' shaggy and black in his lap. Zeb stares at him.

"Watch the road," the guy says again, so Zeb does and then he sneaks a peek and the guy's still there. And he shakes his head and rubs his eyes and remembers to look at the road and the guy's still there.

"Hi. I'm God," the guy says, all friendly and nice.

Zeb starts to tell him he don't look like God, wearing jeans and boots and a torn T-shirt and a John Deere cap over his long hair but then he thinks if this guy ain't God, he don't want to know who else could jest show up in his cab like that and so he shuts up and stares. Until he remembers the road.

Now Zeb ain't never talked to God up close and personal, and he tries not to bother God 'cept for important things. Mebbe later tonight he'll kick himself cause man, what a chance! but right now he's just thinkin' "Shee-yoot!" He can't think of one durn thing to say to a God who looks like a dirty hitchhiker and is holdin' a dead porcupine in his lap.

"Ever see a porcupine?" God asks, finally, and Zeb is tryin' to figger out what to say, rememberin' the BANG! when God smiles a bit and says, "Well, I know you didn't see that one." Zeb relaxes a little, but not much.

God's quiet a bit and then he says, "The quills were difficult. The barbs had to be sharp enough to snag, but at just the right angle. And it was a bit of a decision, deciding on a color. I couldn't decide if they should be white or black, so finally I made them both colors."

God's holdin' out a quill so Zeb takes it but then doesn't know what to do with it so now he's drivin' with a quill in his hand, tryin' to figger out what to say about the stripes that won't sound stupid but God's still talkin'.

"I was kind of proud of the triggering mechanism. I felt it was only fair to give them something to compensate for being so slow and having such a soft belly."

God suddenly shoves the porcupine at Zeb, who is all eyes on the road now, yessir, and says, "Go on, feel his belly. Soft as silk. That wasn't easy either."

Zeb tries to touch the belly and hold the quill and drive and thank – goodness – he don't hit nothin' else. God's quiet now and Zeb looks over and God is strokin' the porcupine's ears and belly and his eyes look damp. Zeb's thinkin' "what the—" and stops himself just in time but God don't seem to notice. Zeb stares through the cracked windshield tryin' to figger out what to say and he finally turns to God, but there ain't no one there, just the porcupine.

Zeb starts thinkin' about makin' things and the good solid

feel of a saw vibratin' in his hands and that sweet spot when the hammer hits the nail just right. And then he thinks about standin' back and lookin' at what he's made and givin' that last solid shake and jest wantin' to show it to someone and maybe a rusted out pickup barrellin' onto the yard out of control …

Zeb stops the truck and gets his shovel outta the back, and some o' them brand-new two-by-fours. He digs a hole right there by the side of the road even though it's gettin' dark. He roots around in the mess on the floor of his truck and finds a grease pencil and writes on one piece of wood and nails the pieces together. He steps back and takes his ball cap off, looks at the cross he's hammered into the dirt:

S – O – R - Y.

# Bearing My Cross

I huddle within this threadbare faith
warm empty hands on a stone-cold heaven
shrink from the possibility
of You being real
and I such a pitiful witness

I long for the warmer, softer garment
of one newly born to faith
enraptured by the celebration
and ceremony of Your church
feasting on the reality
of Your Presence

my life's losses leave me
foraging for crumbs of You
among the starving,
mangled borders
of my dreams

I strain to pray
my tongue grows numb
with grief
I seek to embrace You
my fists are frozen
in anger

I turn away
cast the smoldering
cinders of supplication
towards heaven
oh, this beggared flame
yearns to be rekindled

*Evelyn Heffernan*

# The Hostage

He carries her death with its unborn dreams
from one mourning ritual to the next
savors the aroma of coffee and grief
long after the pot is empty
he roams vacant rooms
rearranges her photographs
flounders in memories
surf-tossed and savage
saltwater invades
his dreams and his bed
upon waking his eyes burn
with the sand of her passage
his arms ache with unfurnished desire
he draws back the sheets
tear-stained and abandoned
gropes for strength to rise
brews the coffee
dons her shroud
falters forward into the day

*Evelyn Heffernan*

# *My Comfort*

you are often the only
rain I receive
in my season
of drought

from your hand
pours living water
- faith -
that quenches me
when I am so parched
with the dust of doubt
I can barely breathe
our Savior's name

your prayers gentle
the desert winds of despair
that scour my arid heart

when your eyes
shine Holy Spirit flame

I need no compass
to lead me to
the oasis of His love

*Evelyn Heffernan*

# Converting to Childhood

*Jesus: "… unless you are converted and become as little children you will by no means enter the Kingdom of Heaven." Matthew 18:3 NASB*

You lose sophistication and veneer
and become clear
sing, skip and play
easily laugh and cry
then fall asleep without a care
for Daddy is nearby.

No longer do you worry
about whether there will be
food to eat, clothes to wear
how to get from here to there.

You're malleable clay again
learning your family's ways and graces.
And once again you fit
into small places.

*Violet Nesdoly*

# A New Vision, A New Understanding

Shirley Kolanchey

IN THE SPRING OF 1990 I WAS diagnosed with an acoustic neuroma (benign brain tumor on the acoustic nerve) and had surgery for it. It brings back some traumatic memories, but I have so many things to be thankful for to do with the actual surgery.

I did not get facial paralysis, my eyes were only affected for a few weeks from my brain swelling. While I did experience cerebrospinal fluid leaking from the brain, it was corrected with no further problem.

Losing my hearing on one side has been one of "life's losses." It can be inconvenient at times but I have learned to try to have people sit on my right; otherwise, I will explain to a person on my left that I can't hear them. My husband, John, has become used to sitting on my deaf side when needed. I can hear fairly well in a group if the people are not sitting too close to me, and if there is no background noise (which does interfere with my hearing). So far, the hearing in my right ear is good.

Sometimes I do have a problem figuring out where sound is coming from, such as if I'm driving a car and I hear a siren, or distinguishing who is speaking to me if there is more than one person around, especially if I don't recognize the voice.

On the positive side, I have become more familiar and interested in both hearing and brain problems, and try to be helpful and sympathetic where possible with others who are similarly affected (one lady lived in New Guinea!). I have learned to adjust to the problems to a fair degree, not only in this area, but in other health problems as well. The word "trauma" has taken on new meaning.

I didn't learn about ANAC until shortly after my operation, but found the newsletters helpful and comforting, especially at first. Some of the personal experiences letters were helpful. In one, the man had been a cyclist, and when he first tried to go back to riding, he fell several times but just kept at it. I applied this to my swimming, overcoming feeling lop-sided and swimming crooked. The first time I tried to swing a golf club, I fell down, and initially had a hard time trying to walk straight in the dark because of loss of balance.

There were a few almost humorous incidents along the way. When I went for my first CAT Scan, I planned to have John accompany me for this important test, but our "best laid plans" went awry. I ended up taking my car to the garage for repairs and got a ride to the hospital in their service van!

My vocabulary shrunk to a couple of words for awhile when reacting to explanations of what was going on. When I asked at the hospital information desk where Dr. Oldring was located and the clerk replied "In surgery," I just exclaimed "He is!" Other times it was "It is" "There is" or "I see" and later when signing all sorts of waiver papers, I was often speechless.

After 7-1/2 hours of surgery and being "out" for 11 hours, I saw John and my sister and several people in white coats. I said hello to John and Eleanor, then asked about our cat (he was diagnosed with diabetes that very day) and whether the Oilers had won the hockey game the night before. My mind was that clear.

While in the hospital I came to appreciate the role of volunteers (one was a high school student and another was an AN survivor), also the staff, as well as many friends who visited.

Every day John would rush in from work with a piece of green paper and say, "Here's the beat," and proceed to read off the names of people who had phoned, and mail received.

After nine days, doctors gave their okay at 7:30 a.m. for me to be discharged. I immediately began to rush around, albeit crawling, as I hadn't had a chance to try walking (John had taken me for a spin around the hospital in a wheelchair the night before) and gathered up my clothes and flowers.

As my friend, Hazel, drove me down the Groat Road and across the bridge, Edmonton's river valley looked its best—the bright sun was shining on fresh green grass and leaves. While I was in the hospital, summer had replaced spring. To me it was as if an era had passed. I was looking at the world with new vision, seeing less, hearing differently, but understanding more.

For the next month, I found great peace in listening to the tape, "The Lord is my Shepherd," by George Beverly Shea, soloist for the Billy Graham Association. A friend had sent it to me just prior to my operation and wrote, "It's my very favorite tape and was a great help to me when I was sick."

My family and friends were praying for me during the operation, and I was on some prayer chains. My Christian faith grew at that time.

While certain after-effects will always be with me, I don't dwell on them or the operation, and trust I am a better person as a result of the experience.

# Living a Healthy Lifestyle – Just Do It

Kimberley Payne

I KNOW THAT GOD CREATED ME AS a whole person and so I need to take care of my whole self. I've learned that there is a direct relationship between my physical, emotional and spiritual health. To become more physically healthy I can exercise, eat nutritionally and stretch my body. I know that practicing healthy living is a way to glorify God. So why don't I do it?

It was only six short months ago that I looked out my living room window to see a gorgeous day outside. Fresh snow covered the landscape and trees were heavy with a blanket of white. The sun reflected off the field in a splash of sparkles – it appeared to be another beautiful winter day. But it was frigid. The thermometer stood at minus twenty Celsius in the sunshine. I cancelled my walk (yet again) because of the cold

For months, my routine was to get my children ready in the morning, walk them to the bus stop and then walk around the neighbourhood by myself. It was a good time to get my body moving, my blood flowing and my mind thinking. On this walk, I practiced my "walking meditation." It was a time when I connected with God and talked to Him through my thoughts and prayers. It was a special time between us that I had come to cherish. On my walks, I explored my life and gave praise and thanksgiving for what He had given me. I opened my heart and poured out my troubles. I gave thought to others and prayed for the needs of my family, friends and community. After my morning walk, I returned home to hot coffee and my pen and paper. I recorded any enlightenment God had shown me, and I reflected on my prayers. It was a time for me to not only talk with God, but to listen for a response.

However, my routine was interrupted when I started a new work schedule and instead of walking to the bus stop I drove the children. Then other days in the week seemed to become busier and I found myself itching to get to my office to clear away the things of yesterday. Instead of starting my day with a walk around the block, I started to weigh it up against other conflicting priorities. The act of walking had to convince me that it was worth it. Each day it was a battle – walk or not walk?

Without this walk, I didn't get my usual energy surge needed for the day. Without this morning boost, I felt like I was dragging myself, and so I also did not have the enthusiasm or desire to do my other exercise – strength training. I was on a downward spiral. Without my morning walk, I not only missed out on the healthy physical benefits, but more importantly I denied the spiritual healing it had provided.

I've learned that prayer, Bible study and journal writing are to my spirit what exercise, healthy eating and stretching are to my body. All require discipline and I need to practice them daily. I know that they are significant in improving balance in my life, improving my quality of life and boosting my mood. They help build healthy relationships; with myself, others and especially God. They can melt tension, reduce stress and provide peace. And with a pure motive, they delight God.

My lesson? Just do it! What I learned is that when I didn't give myself the choice, I went for a walk regardless of temperature or mood. However, when I made walking an option, I had to think each day, *Am I up to it? Do I have time for it? Is it warm enough or cool enough or dry enough?* Each day I put myself through a dance of questions, instead of just doing it.

"Just do it" (the saying made famous by Nike) has tremendous impact. If I would just walk in the morning, instead of giving myself the option, I would not have to worry about what is more important on my list of things to do. I would return from my walk refreshed and ready to face the day. A healthy body would give me the energy and enthusiasm to carry out the purposes that God has for my life. I need to be faithful about doing something each day in order to realize the full potential of God's plan for me.

It is no longer snowy and cold outside and I can enjoy summer fitness once again. It's open to nature hikes and family bike rides; spur-of-the-moment volleyball games on the back lawn, and lots of swimming; summer gardening and bug catching with the kids. There are no rules. There is no clock.

I am invited to take a fresh physical and spiritual attitude on a daily basis. God created my body to be built for action. Therefore, activity is needed to keep me fit. His law in nature is to exercise, eat right, and serve Him. I need to take care of myself and obey the law of nature. Taking care of myself physically is one way to honour God with my body.

*Don't you know that you yourselves are God's temple and that God's Spirit lives in you?* (1 Corinthians 3:16 NIV)

# The Homecoming

Glynis M. Belec

"WHAT HAPPENED TO YOUR HAIR, Grandma?" Trenton asked as he rubbed his chubby fingers over my fuzzy head.

"Do you mean why does my head feel funny?"

I hugged my sweetheart grandson a little closer.

My locks and even a few eyebrows and lashes are starting to make an appearance now that my chemotherapy treatments are finished, thank goodness. At first, getting used to being hairless was a bit of a stretch for this vain old gal.

Eventually, though, I got used to it and I really don't mind going without a hat, even in public now. I definitely never wear a chapeau of any description within my own walls. Too hot. Too bothersome. Too indicative that vanity still gnaws.

It's been almost six months since my locks departed. That's a significant portion of 3-year-old Trenton's life when I think about it. Grandma without hair has been the norm for a while. So as he ran his little fingers along the top of my head yesterday, Trenton got a bit of a surprise.

"Grandma's hair is starting to grow back," I told the little munchkin.

Trenton looked at me with that irresistible grin and then stroked my head once again and made the most precious statement: "Grandma. Your hair is coming back home!"

So there I have it. My hair as it slowly emerges really is coming home to roost - right on top of my head. And for that I am grateful. I'm not particularly fond of the hue, however I keep telling myself - at least it's hair.

I remember when Trenton asked me what happened to my hair when I lost it as a result ofthe chemotherapy back in June. I wrote a poem for Trenton entitled "Where is Grandma's Hair?"

Here's a taste:

Where is Grandma's Hair?

I looked in the bathroom
I looked behind the chair
I looked in the cupboard
Where is Grandma's hair?

I looked in my bedroom
I looked in my bed
I'm worried about Grandma
There's no hair on her head.

I called up the doctor
On my plastic phone
But he would not answer
There was no dial tone.

I looked in the laundry room
I looked on the shelf
I looked in the basket
I can't find it myself.

So I went up to Mommy
And asked her what was wrong

"Grandma's hair has disappeared –
It used to be so long."

"Grandma has a sickness,"
Mommy's face looked sad.
"The doctor called it cancer
But the news isn't bad."

"When Grandma went to hospital
The doctor said, 'Don't fret.'
We'll give her some medicine
No need to be upset."

I went into Grandma's room
She was wearing a hat
She gave me a hug and asked,
"Shall we have a chat?"

'Yes," I told my Grandma
"Where is your hair?
I have looked in every room
I even said a prayer."

"The medicine the doctor gives,
Sometimes makes me sick,
My hair fell out but then he said,
'It will soon grow back in thick.'"

Then Grandma told me something else
She said, "Come over here."
She winked and opened up a drawer
And then she pulled me near.

I did not need to search again
For Grandma's long, lost hair
When I looked inside the drawer
I laughed at what was there.

Grandma called them "hair hats"
Blonde, black, brown and red
Wigs - of every size and shape
To cover her bald head!

# *Finding Fulfillment*

Jan Keats

*"I will listen to God the Lord. He has ordered peace for those who worship Him!"* (Psalm 85:8 NIV)

MY DAUGHTER AND I LOVE TO shop together. One occasion made me realize that shopping wasn't just something to do, it was a bonding time between a mother and daughter.

At a clothing store, we had picked out a few articles and proceeded to the change rooms. We found stalls next to each other and were soon engaged in a wonderful chat about our findings, among other things. Suddenly we heard a voice from the adjacent stall saying, "You two must be mother and daughter."

We both acknowledged that we were. Then the mysterious elderly lady's voice said somberly, "I never had a daughter; listening to you both makes me wish that I had. You seem to be really close. I have a son whom I love dearly, but my son doesn't like to shop." She chuckled.

We were speechless, hoping to say something to appease her sorrowful and unfulfilled heart. At the same time we realized how grateful we were to have a special mother/daughter relationship. Neither of us saw that elderly woman. She left the change room before we did. We were having too much fun trying on clothes.

Throughout the rest of the day, we couldn't get that woman off our minds. *She must be so lonely*, I thought. I wondered if she had found fulfillment in life. We didn't know anything about her, yet our hearts ached for her. Was she widowed? Was she living all alone? Does her son live nearby? Did she browse the shopping centres frequently to fill the void in her life? Did she know God? We simply didn't know.

But God knows. The woman was blessed with a son, yet she hoped to have had a daughter to bond with. The woman was also blessed with a long life, yet it seemed she was feeling empty and unfulfilled in her senior years. Even through her blessings, she had a longing for peace.

The Bible says that God is the peace and joy giver. His promises are for her. His uncompromising peace is for her. Psalm 5:11a (NIV) says, "But let all who take refuge in you be glad; let them ever sing for joy."

How about you? Are you content and at peace with God? Fulfillment comes through trusting and walking daily with God. Your life is carved into his hand. As I remember the lonely woman, and how I was caused to feel her emptiness, I pray that she will find the peace and contentment she is longing for. Proverbs 30:5 (NIV) says, "Every word of God is flawless; He is a shield to those who take refuge in Him."

Lord, help us to seek and find fulfillment when we feel empty and lonely. We believe you are the true source of life, who offers peace and joy to everyone.

Amen.

# Something Stinks

Ruth L. Snyder

*"But if you fail to do this, you will be sinning against the Lord; and you may be sure that your sin will find you out."*
Numbers 32:23 NIV

"THE VAN STINKS," MY HUSBAND said. He emphasized his distaste by screwing up his face.

"It was fine yesterday." I shrugged. "I don't know why it would stink today."

My husband hastily carried a can of Lysol out to the van to do battle with the unwanted smell. Minutes later, our family entered the "stinky" van. As we drove to camp to pick up our daughter, my husband updated me on the progress he was making with his "to do" list. "By the way, when was the last time I changed oil?"

I pushed the button on the glove box. Just as I was about to slide my hand in to pull out our maintenance book, I spotted a small, brown, furry creature. Its beady, lifeless eyes stared back at me. I gasped. "Eeeew! No wonder it stinks in here."

"What?"

"This." I gingerly pulled out the book and showed him the partially decomposed body of a mouse. Then I hurled the intruder out the nearest window.

My husband chuckled. "It smells better in here already."

Later that day, I thought about that dead mouse and how much it affected the atmosphere of our van, even though no one could see it. Then I thought about how we sometimes make bad choices that have devastating results. Often we allow sin into our lives, thinking that no one will notice. *After all, it's just a thought,* we may reason. *It's just a little "white lie." It won't hurt anyone.*

However, sin is sin. Eventually our choices will make themselves known. Our sin will start to "stink," affecting our relationship with God and others. Perhaps that "innocent" thought will become a bad habit that takes years to break. Perhaps others will start to distrust us because we often lie to them. Perhaps that lingering glance will be the first step down the hurtful path of sexual sin and eventual divorce.

Just as I had to get rid of the dead mouse to escape the smell, so also we need to allow God to deal with the sin in our lives to get rid of its evil effects. The first step is recognizing our sin. Then we need to acknowledge that it is wrong and decide not to allow it into our life any more. Finally, we need to confess and forsake our sins, hidden or open.

What "stink" do I need to deal with today? If I will allow God to get rid of my "stinky" sin, my life can instead become a pleasing aroma to those around me.

*Dear Heavenly Father, Thank you that you know my secret sins. Forgive me for ______________. I acknowledge that it is not pleasing to you and ask you to make me clean. Amen.*

# Life Goes On

Mary Haskett

Ellie stood at her bedroom window. The rumble of a truck now parked outside the "sold" house across the street had piqued her curiosity.

"Mommy, Andy see."

She smiled down at her three-year-old son. His plump little arms stretched out towards her.

"Okay Pumpkin, " she said, swinging him up onto her hip.

"Tuck Andy see."

"Yes little buddy." She buried her face in his neck and smothering it with kisses. Her son's laughter made her laugh too. As she straightened up she saw a tall young man watching them. He acknowledged her with a slight nod and then proceeded to unload the truck, sliding a pair of gleaming white water skis, with a red stripe running down the centre of each, to the ground. A small gasp escaped her lips and she remembered once more.

*It's as if he's placing my Mark there,* she thought. Her stomach churned. She saw it all vividly: her husband's head bobbing uncontrollably in the lake. He'd been surfacing from the water to ski again. His friend Trevor had revved up the engine, when in one terrible moment a small high powered craft seemed to appear from nowhere, striking the back of Mark's head. She heard the screams, her screams and other people's screams.

She saw hands holding him up—frantic, not sure what to do. She saw Mark's pale face and his eyes that had been displaced by the force of the blow, so that only the whites showed. Then there was the red, the red that never stopped, streaming out of the back of his head, swirling and whirling in the wake of the aftermath; the seemingly endless struggle of glistening sun-soaked bodies carrying Mark and placing him on the sand. Then death; and she, heavy with child, slumped onto the sand, praying it was a nightmare. Far above the plaintive cries of seagulls floated down in mournful chorus.

People around her, some at the water's edge and others on the beach, moved in slow motion. All sound was distant. Her father lifted her up and together they stumbled up the beach to her mother.

The ringing of the phone brought Ellie back to the present. Andy, who had been watching the unloading of the truck, struggled to be free.

"Andy get."

Ellie let him slide down on to the bed behind her. Within seconds he announced into the mouthpiece, "Mommy come." Ellie took the phone and sat on the side of the bed, glancing at her reflection in the mirror. Her green eyes focused on her dark brown hair. *I need a trim,* she thought. She pushed it back from her face and lay back on the pillows as she responded to her friend's greeting.

"Hi Jenny," she said in a small voice.

"What's up, Ellie?"

"It happened again. I saw it all, the blood, Just horrible."

Jenny spoke softly, "Still going on." For a moment silence stood between them.

"Jen, are you there?" Ellie's voice trembled.

"I'm here, Ellie. I'm thinking it happens so often, I mean you reliving the accident. If you could bring yourself to come to the lake, I believe it might help and you could enjoy the water again. That's why I'm calling. Ann and I are taking the kids for a picnic lunch and…"

"No! I'm not coming." Ellie interjected.

"The same as last time," Jenny said.

"That's right and don't ask me to the lake again, Jen."

"What about Andy? He'd love the beach."

"Stop it, Jen! Don't try hanging guilt trips on me."

"Okay, but it's not what I'm trying to do," Jenny said gently. "If you change your mind, we'll be on that stretch of beach in front of the parking lot."

"You don't care."

"I do, but I can't stay back there with you. Life goes on Ellie. 'Bye for now ."

After the click, Ellie lay there and listened to the line hum. A tear trickled down her face. Why was Jenny so insensitive? Of course she could not go to the lake—ever. Supposing another accident happened. She shuddered, replaced the receiver and called to Andy.

Downstairs she busied herself with preparing breakfast. Andy's chatter put a smile back on her face. With great determination he climbed into his high-chair.

"Andy Barton, mommy loves you," Ellie said as she placed a bowl of cereal on his tray. She sat down and watched him. Her thoughts drifted to Jenny as she sipped her coffee. *But I can't go*, she thought, *I just can't*. The soft chimes of the doorbell interrupted her reverie.

"No, little guy," she said to Andy as he tried to climb out of his high-chair. "I'll be right back." She moved quickly down the passageway and opened the front door.

"Oh, the man with the skis."

He smiled a warm smile that came right from his dark brown eyes and turned his mouth up slightly on the left side. "Hi, Brett Melnick, your new neighbor." He held out a large hand.

"Ellie Barton." She placed her hand in his and a few seconds later wriggled her fingers free from his firm grasp. She waited for him to speak, resentment welling up within her. He had reminded her of Mark's death.

"Could you lend me some milk?" he asked. "I forgot to get some and I can't manage without coffee at least every four hours."

Ellie managed a weak smile. "Sure, step inside. I'll be back in a moment." As she walked to the kitchen she struggled with her emotions. She knew it was wrong to feel hostility towards the guy who had unwittingly caused a renewal of her pain. After all, he didn't know about Mark. *Besides,* she thought as she opened the fridge door, *how many times did something happen that triggered memories of Mark*?

Back at the front door she handed him a bag of milk.

"I'll replace it tomorrow if that's okay." For a moment his eyes held hers. She felt her heart skip a beat.

"Sure, no problem," she said trying to sound matter-of-fact. "Are you new to the area or moving from another part of the village?"

"Brand new. And you?"

"I've been here four years since... since I married." Her voice faltered.

"Guess I'll meet your other half sometime."

"My husband died three years ago."

"I'm sorry," Brett said quietly.

Suddenly she smiled. "Well, it's been a while now and life goes on you know."

"You are so right. Life goes on." For a moment his eyes registered sadness and Ellie sensed he struggled too. She cleared her throat.

"If you'll excuse me, I have to get going. I'm meeting some friends at the lake."

Brett nodded. " I'll see you tomorrow." He hesitated, then

added. "I look forward to seeing you tomorrow."

"Me too," she said.

In the kitchen Ellie announced to Andy, "We're going to the lake. That's what I said and that's what we'll do." She pulled rolls, cold meats and mayonnaise from the fridge and rummaged in the crisper for fruit. Half an hour later, with Andy strapped in his car seat chatting to his teddy, Ellie pushed on the accelerator as she left the village and hit the highway toward the lake. *I can hardly believe I'm doing this.*

The warmth of the sun and the summer breeze blowing through the open window lifted her spirits. In her mind over and over again, she heard Jenny saying "Life goes on" and she had repeated it to Brett and he had echoed it back to her. That small phrase had caused her to take stock of herself. "Thanks guys," she whispered. Tears glistened in her eyes, but she smiled broadly. *It's like coming out of a long dark tunnel.*

# God Never Sleeps

should a bed represent terror?
for me it is a symbol like a serpent
or tongued gargoyle
an open cavern to hell
or beyond

filled with memories
staining the created order
marring that part of humanity that groans for redemption
streaking the mind
with nightmares inescapable

clamoring for control until the last moment
I surrender at last to pounding fear
wishing there was some other way
to face the night than going to bed

if only a mattress meant peace not
turmoil comfort not
wringing release not
combat

God never sleeps

what has that to do with me?
it seemed He slept, years ago, when this bed became a rack

seeming is not being.
He slept not then. He sleeps not now. He sleeps not
in the future.

can an oven of coals become an altar?
does God drive demons from their places? heal memories that cannot be touched with gauze?
take fear and strangle it in a Warrior vise until it expires as leviathan writhing in the sand and gasping its last?

God never sleeps

*Wayne Bos*

# African Proverb

those who have teeth find no meat
those who have none have too much

I fed your son his first cheeseburger
I drove your wife to the country
to escape the pressure
                    of divorce proceedings

I bought your child electrolyte
allowing him to vomit on my shirt
while you expended your lasciviousness
                    on worthless women

you had a bride
          who would have died in faithfulness
you traded it all for a manipulator
                              who will leave you
                                    as your health fails

why does a man walk away
from what another pleads to God for
all his life
and cannot have?

perhaps the day will come
when God will bring meat
to a man with teeth

*Wayne Bos*

# Happy Birthday

You're invited to a party –
  It's the birthday of a King!
There'll be lots of fun and laughter,
  Games to play and songs to sing.
We'll give presents to each other,
  Lavish gifts that we don't need;
And we'll eat until we waddle
  Blatant in our festive greed.

We'll spend days in preparation…
  Buying, wrapping, running 'round,
Till the still small voice of Jesus
  Is by all the chaos drowned.
Since it is His birthday party
  Maybe we should stop to hear,
After all, this celebration
  Happens only once a year!

What would Jesus say, I wonder,
  If He tangibly were here?
Would He be impressed with us,
  And with our great array of cheer?
Or would He have to clear the temple
  As He did so long ago?
Angered by our greed and getting,
  Saddened by our shallow show.

Lord, forgive me for forgetting
    You are why the angels came.
You are Who the wisemen worshipped;
    Help me now to do the same.
King of Kings and Lord of Lords,
    Born to die that I might live.
Happy birthday, precious Saviour,
    My life, the gift to You I give.

*Elizabeth Volk*

# His Footprints Are Not Seen

Confused, I look ahead of me
  And see view a mighty, raging sea
    This is His way? It cannot be!

      His footprints are not seen.

I feel confusion, fear, and doubt
  The way seems dark, with no way out
    :"Where are You, Lord?" I fret and shout

      His footprints are not seen.

Just when I'm tempted to let go
  He comes to me, and lets me know
    He loves me, and is there, although

      His footprints are not seen.

Sometimes His path leads through the sea
  But I know His way's best for me
    "By faith, not sight," His face I see.

      His footprints are not seen.

*"Your path led through the sea, Your way through the mighty waters, though Your footprints were not seen."*
(Psalm 77:19, NIV)

*Elizabeth Volk*

# *The Zipper*

Frances Ruiter

TELEPHONE CALL ON A MONDAY morning. 9:15 am. A woman asks for Greta.

"Here she is." I hand over the phone to my dearest wife, Greta. I continue to read my book, paying no further attention to the conversation.

After putting the phone down, Greta says, "That was Rosally. She asked if I would mind taking her husband along on my usual walk around the perimeter of our Senior Citizen Home." (Our building is a large complex surrounded by a road and sidewalk)

Rosally is not able to walk very far and explained that her husband, Arnold, has Alzheimer's. "I don't trust him to go alone for fear he will get lost." Greta told her she was happy to walk along with him and would be ready to go in a few minutes and would meet him at 9:30 at the front entrance.

So there they go. Greta leading, walking at a nice pace. They make three rounds, a total distance of almost three kilometers. This takes about a half an hour. When I asked her later how she made out, she replied, "Oh, it was okay, He slowed down a while but he picked up the pace again when I spurred him on."

Arnold is always very happy to see Greta; he is excited to go for a walk and generally keeps up with her. Sometimes he is a bit late having breakfast and Greta takes a peek in the dining room to see if he is there. When he does see her, he jumps up from his chair, gets his jacket, and heads for the front entrance, and off they go. One day Arnold mentioned that he told his son that he walked with a nice lady.

Greta thought that was amusing. Another time he told her he thought she was amazing, making her blush.

I was not concerned about their walking together. Arnold needed company and seemed to be a kind fellow, and I was happy that Greta could be a walking companion for him. He is about my age and almost bald, but in fairly good shape. Actually I didn't pay much thought to the fact that the two of them went out for a stroll a few times a week.

Then, one day. Greta mentioned, in passing, that while she was about ready to go for a walk with Arnold, he needed assistance with his zipper. Zipper?

"What zipper?" I asked slyly. Suddenly, I was very much alert.

"It was his coat, dummy! He couldn't get the zipper to work."

"Oh, I see," and I grinned.

However, it did leave me a little bit more curious. The next time I saw Arnold, I took a closer look at him, to see what shape he was in and whether he could look me straight in the eye. Ha, all is well; Greta is doing good work, full of grace in service to her neighbour and friend.

A week later Greta mentioned that she showed Arnold her latest drawing of two ice bears displayed in the art room of our building. He thought it was fantastic: "You are a great artist." Then, as she is directing him to the elevator to get to his apartment, he gives her a hug, and says, "You are a very nice person."

When she told me this story with some hesitation and wondered how I would react to that, I told her that Arnold is right. "I agree with him, That is the reason why I love you. Now let's go to bed."

# How to Survive the Doubts and Droughts of Writing Life

Sulochana Vinayagamoorthy

If asked, each of us has an interesting story to tell how we got into the business of writing. As in any business, writing comes with challenges that need to be thought through, planned out and prayed about to stay afloat and succeed. During the course, self-doubts and discouragements may collide with our interest and make us want to quit. Unfortunately, some novice writers give up at this stage without giving themselves a chance to prove their potential to flourish. The rest, meanwhile, plow through seasons of doubts and droughts and thrive to see their work in print.

Do Not Allow Self-Doubt To Rob Your Dream

It took awhile for us to admit to ourselves and to others that we are writers. We find it easy to acknowledge others' talents and achievements. But, when encouraged to submit our work to the publishers or called to read out our manuscript to a circle of writers, we cower in self-doubt and let the opportunity to succeed pass us by. Comparing our writing with that of those who had published for years, we further question our ability to get published. Interestingly, the concept of talent is misunderstood to an extent that it had energized some to excel in their pursuit, and allowed others to wade in a comfort zone, producing nothing to display.

History reveals that success is guaranteed only to those who persist and permit themselves to perspire. Try not to say to yourself, "I've nothing interesting to say," or "no one wants to read my work anyway." Listen not and believe not those who are quick to find flaws in your writing. Instead, meet up with those who show genuine interest in your progress, listen to their critiquing, and hone your skill as best as you can. Even well known authors do doubt their ability to write when starting on a new book, breaking into a different genre or taking up a challenging assignment. So, be encouraged and keep on writing.

Grow Up!

Rejections do sting, and make us cry with self-pity. Receiving rejections reflects your intent to publish. So, pat yourself for your effort and be proud of what you create. Editors are on the lookout for promising newcomers. They reject manuscripts that do not suit their market, not the writers who wrote them. Hence, prove to them your commitment and get through the door to get published.

Cast Away Those Writer's Blues

Creativity surely takes a toll on the brain- our creative well. Seasons of despair and dryness intervene in every writer's life. "I think the artist spirit definitely needs refreshing, perhaps more often than most other occupations," says Linda Anderson, the author of *Interludes.* She further adds, "Embracing a desert time is more healthy and helpful and effective than resisting and forcing yourself to write stilted, cobwebby phrases and wooden words." She seemed to have learned such wisdom the hard way. After being in writing for twenty years and amidst her busy schedules of writing and speaking engagements, a bout of cancer urged her to slow down. She stopped writing altogether when her Interlude manuscript got rejected twenty-five times. She, then, started to make handmade greeting cards with pressed flowers.

"My strength began to return. My creative well was filled back up without me even realizing it," she writes. Because writing is an intensive introspective work, Anderson encourages writers to take an artist's break one day a month or few hours a day to rejuvenate the body and the spirit.

During the lull period when your energy measures low and ideas smell stale, you could do the following to shoo away the blues.

Repackage and resell your published stories.

Read through your old journals and unearth new topics for future writing. Research new markets; study the style, layout and content. Read great books with writer's eyes and improve your writing skill.

Yield Not To Perfectionism

"A perfect poem is impossible. Once it had been written, the world would end." Robert Graves.

Perfectionism is a malady some of us encounter on a daily basis. By raising the bar of expectation on ourselves, we delete, cross out or rewrite the sentence for the nth time before we could even put down our thoughts in the first paragraph of the first draft. The fear of not being able to put our brilliant thought in a perfect story stiffens our fingers and interrupts our chain of thought. Such high expectation results in a writer's block. An author who used to deny the existence of writer's block came to face to face with it when she tried to write a letter to the woman who was carrying the baby the author planned to adopt. She wanted to write a perfect letter, pouring all her love for the unborn baby and expressing her gratitude to the woman who chose her to adopt the child. To her surprise, she found herself staring at the screen, and being unable to type out even a single sentence.

When you start writing your first draft, give no thought to whether you can sell it, " be good enough" for anyone to like it or even worth your time to write it. Your job is to put down your thoughts onto the paper as much as possible, and as soon as possible. If you still find yourself editing your work no sooner than you have typed your first sentence, try another approach to download your thoughts. Perhaps, writing it in longhand would help. You could also dictate it onto a tape recorder and transcribe it later. Those who continue to wrestle with perfectionism could benefit by using software like "Dragon" which allows you to dictate directly onto your computer. Editors are looking for well-written manuscripts, not perfect ones. Practice makes you a better writer, even if you are not aware of the improvement immediately. So, practice, practice, practice!

# The Chrysalis of Time

Eulene Hope Moores

IN MY KITCHEN I HAVE BUTTERFLIES.

On my walls, fridge, dishes, plants, bookmarks - and stickers for everything.

The reason I love Butterflies is that I love what they represent. The saga of a Butterfly has always fascinated me and, since I found that the word *metamorphosis* comes from a Greek word that describes *my* saga as well, I was more than fascinated; I was captivated!

The fact that a tiny, often ugly, earth-bound, limited, caterpillar could ever become the beautiful air-borne butterfly that we all love to watch, is almost beyond comprehension. I've tried to imagine what changes must take place inside that hard, dead chrysalis hanging from the branch! It is inconceivable that it could contain anything living, or that such enormous change could be happening inside. Yet, in due time, that exquisite creature emerges, dries its newly formed wings, and flutters away into the blue yonder.

*Metamorphosis* is the word used to describe this transformation. It is used four times in the New Testament. Both Matthew and Mark use it to describe the *transfiguration* of Jesus when His appearance was changed in the company of Peter, James and John on the mountain.

Paul, writing to the Church at Rome, admonished them to

not be conformed to this world, but to be *transformed (metamorphosed)* by the renewing of their minds. *(Rom. 12:2 NKJV)*

This is the verse that captivates me: "But we all, with unveiled face, beholding as in a mirror the glory of the Lord, are being *transformed (metamorphosed)* into the same image from glory to glory, just as by the Spirit of the Lord." *(2 Cor. 3:18 NKJV)* "We all" includes you! And me! As we behold God's glory, in whatever form it is presented to us, it changes us.

The Scriptures tell us that God set out in the beginning to make man(kind) in His image. He has not changed His mind, nor His plan, nor His determined purpose to accomplish this most incredible, miraculous undertaking. As the Master Planner and Designer that He is, He is steadily and faithfully working to complete the work He began. We are assured that God has subjected His creation to the vicissitudes of this Chrysalis of Time in order to develop His highest creation. Of that creation, believers, in a living relationship with Jesus Christ, are individual members in which He has placed His Spirit. We have been foreordained to be *conformed (metamorphosed)* to the image of God's Son. *(Rom. 8:29 NKJV)*

We are told that we are His Workmanship into which He is infusing His Divine nature. And it is being done "precept upon precept, line upon line, line upon line, here a little, there a little" … "till we all come…to the measure of the stature of the fullness of Christ." We are promised that "as we have borne the image of the man of dust, we shall also bear the image of the heavenly Man." *(Isa. 28:10; Eph. 4:13; 1 Cor. 15:49 NKJV)*

"Beloved," says the Apostle John, "now we are the children of God, and it has not yet been revealed what we shall be, but we know that when He is revealed," (and we emerge from our 'chrysalis' in resurrection life) "*we shall be like Him,* for we shall see Him as He is. And every one who has this hope (confident expectation) in Him purifies himself, even as He is pure."*(1 John 3:2,3 NKJV)*

Something that I recently discovered: in the metamorphosis of the caterpillar to the butterfly, *only the internal organs remain the same!* That lends new meaning to: "Therefore, if anyone is in Christ, he is a new creation; old things have passed away; behold, all things have become new!" *(2 Cor. 5:17 NKJV)* Being new creations in Christ Jesus and having His Spirit dwelling within, only that nature of Christ will remain, while all the old externals shall be done away.

Charles Wesley put it well in this verse from his well-known hymn, Love Divine:

Finish then Thy new creation, pure and spotless let us be;
Let us see Thy great salvation perfectly restored in Thee.
*Changed from glory into glory,* till in heav'n we take our place,
Till we cast our crowns before Thee, lost in wonder, love and praise.

Understanding that we are presently in the process of that grand Spiritual Metamorphosis, being transformed from earthy to heavenly, we should not then be surprised when we sometimes feel imprisoned by the circumstances in which we find ourselves; when we feel restrained by our human limitations; when we greatly desire to be liberated from the 'chrysalis' that confines us; when our hearts long for something more than our minds can define.

I have tried to express the thought in the following lines which I call "The Chrysalis of Time:"

You have confined me in this Chrysalis of Time
To work Your Sovereign will and purpose so sublime;
To give to me Your life, my spirit to renew;
To change me from within; to make me more like You;
Transformed by Grace Divine into Your image fair,
I shall come forth at last, Your Glory then to share.

Then let us lift up our heads "and rejoice in hope of the Glory of God." *(Rom. 5:2 NKJV)*

# Santa Claws

Barbara Quaale

"THAT'S IT! I'VE HAD IT! THAT cat's got to go!" my roomie screamed.

BJ wasn't a bad cat. Not smart enough to be bad. A fat washed out ginger with even paler cream stripes, he, unfortunately, wasn't smart enough to know the chimney didn't qualify as an approved exit either. He sat on the slate hearth, in his new sooty suit, shaking his head and twitching his ears in a perplexed fashion. Black dust drifted down all over Marabella's fine white Christmas decorations. They looked like they'd been through a dust storm from Hell.

"My writer's group arrives in five minutes! Look what that creature's done!" she ranted.

"Look what your chimney's done!" I answered. "Maybe a cosmic hint you should clean it! 'Sides, nobody's going to care. You have cookies." Marabella did have cookies. Little iced confections that'd break your heart to eat, but break you more not to.

"Get that animal out of here!" she said. I picked BJ up, ignoring my new Christmas t-shirt. Funny how when you love someone, dirt doesn't matter so much. I tucked BJ away and closed my door.

"Look, I'll get the vacuum," I said. "It'll be fine."

"Good. You do that!" she answered and swept off to the kitchen to torture more icing.

Christmas decorations. Bleh! Cutesy art so sweet it would make Wal-mart proud. Sparkling snowmen and cabbage-face kids in precise semicircles around an ice pond, toy shop and stable thingy. I set to with the vacuum, carefully extracting imperfection from fake snow. Working…Looking good!

Kaklopmph!

Uh-oh.

I glanced over my shoulder. Marabella clattered around the kitchen. Desperately, I scanned scenery. Everything seemed intact. The little stable thingy had all its parts: sheep, cows, camels for the wise guys…oh, snap! The baby was missing! I looked up the tube. Why do we do that, anyway? Like it's still going to be there or something. The suction tugged on my eyebrow chain.

BING-BONG!!

"Get that in the closet!" Marabella hissed as she swept into the room. "And change your shirt!" I rolled my eyes. These stupid do's. *Everything* had to pass inspection. You'd think writers had never seen dirt before. Well, maybe these guys hadn't. Was some church group after all. I brushed at the smudges. No dice.

BJ jumped off the dresser as I pulled out a fresh tee. Oops. AC/DC. Last tour. That wouldn't do. KISS? Nope. Judas Priest? Definitely not. Alice Cooper? She'd never invite me again. Prism. Yeah. That'd work. Nice rainbow on the shades. Wasn't there something about rainbows in the Bible? I squirmed into it.

"And this is my roommate, Addy," Marabella glowed, waving a manicured hand my way. Scary nails, even when not painted Christmas red. You'd never know my cat had just massacred her décor. "Addy writes poetry…well, songs, really." Her smile froze a little. Her eyes darted from my face, to my shirt and back again. Marabella never did know quite how to translate me to her other friends.

"WRROWWERRR!" That was all the warning we got. Tinkle.

Tinkle, tinkle, SWISH! CRASH!!! Down came the Christmas tree, right on top of Marabella's friends, knocking one flat. Big tree. Glass ornaments too. Mirrored shards sprayed everywhere. BJ climbed from the wreckage festooned in tinsel with a shattered Santa head hooked on his ear. Very Punk. He gave a stunned meow. I scooped him up.

Marabella…exploded.

Lose the sound track, it would have been fun to watch. Her eyebrows crinkled down, hands came up in claws. Her eyes got so wide the eyeliner parted in the corners. I swear her hair expanded like a mad scientist's. Then came the words. Her friends just stared.

"You stupid head-banger loser! You ruin everything! Can't you keep that fleabag under control?! All my ornaments! All my work! Don't you care about anything but yourself? Why do you always mess everything up?! First the hearth scene, now—" She stopped, dead quiet. I cringed. The other thing about Marabella was her eye for detail. Probably something to do with the cookie thing. She looked from the hearth to me. One red painted claw pointed, trembling. I stroked BJ's head nervously.

"Where…is…JESUS?!" she said, each word louder than the last. I opened my mouth. The victim of the tree slaying finally extracted herself, pulling ornament hooks and needles from her sweater. She cleared her throat and gave Marabella a pointed look.

"Good question," she said.

I closed my mouth. Turns out I didn't have to say a thing.

# The Watergiver

Dorothy Bentley

THE NOONDAY HEAT OF SAMARIA pressed down on Tama, making her feel lightheaded. Her husband had left the day before on another trip to trade his wares. Maybe this time he would make enough so they could move.

Tama went to the water pot and saw there was only one ladleful of stagnant liquid.

"Put your tablets away and go outside," Tama said to her sons. "I'm too thirsty to do anything."

"But Mama," began Reuben.

"No buts or I'll take a rod to you! If only your father knew how you are both like the Assyrians who terrorized our people, he would not expect me to teach you." Tama lay on her mat.

"Come on," Nathan said to his brother Reuben, glaring over his shoulder. The boys' voices drifted off and Tama's eyes closed.

"This place—I am so tired of living in Samaria. It is always dusty, and those vile Samaritans, those half-breeds who claim to have God's truth, rule the city. If only we could move back to Judea so Nathan and Reuben could attend Synagogue along with the rest of God's true followers."

There was a bang on the door.

"Tama! Are you home?"

"Who is it?" Tama called without getting up.

"It's me, Lysa. My husband fell. Can you come and help? I have no one to watch my babies."

"No, I can't come. I'm too thirsty. I am almost out of water, and I want to be wise with the little I have."

"Why don't you go to the well and get more?"

"I can't right now. Go away so I can rest."

Tama closed her eyes. She recalled earlier days when a stream flowed beside her house. It had flowed with such abundance. Tama had loved the sound of gurgling water and would listen to the melody. She'd cup her hands and take sweet handfuls to drink. She had never known what it was like to thirst.

"There was nothing but time then," bemoaned Tama to herself. "I didn't have little terrorists then to keep me from the waters. Besides, I remember what it was like having abundance. I remember the sounds and the taste. I remember how refreshed I was. I will content myself with the memory. I have trained myself to make do with little."

As Tama had gone to the stream less frequently, the waters had dwindled. Tama barely noticed until one day when passing by on an errand, she noticed the streambed was completely dry. "This is a cursed place," she'd said.

Tama resorted to filling her pot once a week at the well. She always went early Sunday morning, but she'd not gone for weeks. She was tired the first week and decided to stay home. But by the second week, Tama was exhausted and couldn't possibly go. Now, many weeks later, she was in such a state of fatigue that she didn't think she could ever go again.

"Tama!" A piercing yell made Tama sit bolt upright. A scarlet cloth blazed by the window. The woman didn't stop. Tama was glad. It was a prostitute.

"Young men, old men! Listen to me! I met One who told me

everything I ever did. He is the Watergiver! He said He would give me water so I would never thirst again; water that would spring up into eternal life!"

A jolt ran though Tama's body. She suddenly felt desperate to find the Watergiver.

"I need that water," Tama said to herself. "I have to go and find Him. I am tired of being thirsty all the time." Tama forced herself to get up.

"Nathan! Reuben!" Tama went outside. "Where are you? I have to go out."

"Here, Mama," waved Nathan. "Is it okay if we stay and help our neighbours take care of their babies? Look, Reuben is teaching them."

"When did this happen?"

"When did what happen?" asked Nathan.

"When did you both become useful? Never mind. I'll be back in a little while." Tama pulled on her head covering as she followed the crowd to the well.

The Watergiver stayed in the city for two days teaching. As the days and the weeks passed, Tama visited the well regularly. Eventually her strength returned and she taught her boys to fetch water.

One day, Tama thought of the stream she had loved. She went down to the dry bed and just sat. She returned often, and talked with the Watergiver as He often met her there. She began singing to Him, here and there, and He enjoyed it. Before long, a trickle of water began in the streambed.

Tama began singing at her chores and smiling again. And when someone came to her door, Tama always had an extra cup of fresh water to give. The clay of her water pot never dried.

One day, she heard her husband at the door, hesitating. Tama met him with a smile and a warm embrace.

"Father!" Nathan and Reuben threw their arms around him, too.

After a satisfying supper, they reclined on their mats.

"Thank you, husband, for your hard work to give us this home. And look at your sons… they are always helpful now."

Tama's husband grinned. "It's good to be home."

# Soul Food

This sun-shimmering day is a time
for squirreling away memories
to feed my soul in winter.
I will feast on the sight of mighty monarchs
silent sentinels guarding the sacred beauty
of the hidden valley.

I will recall glistening glaciers
and dazzling snow capped peaks.
I will hold in my heart the sight of
brilliant larches, and bright gold aspens
shining in dark forests.

Memories that make my spirit dance
like leaping waves and stillness of the deep,
like wind on rippling waters,
like the changing shades
of emerald and jade, of indigo and umber.

Memories of this beauty
remind me of you, Creator God,
who formed both land and sea
and found them very good.

*Gwyneth Bell*

# Trust Your Pilot

Is your life encountering turbulence
    Over which you have no control?
Are you jostled and buffeted about
    By the stormy winds that blow?
Then remember there is a Pilot
    Who will guide you safely through
Until the troubling storms are spent
    If you will just ask Him to.

Is your life enveloped in darkness
    With no flicker of hope in view?
Are you groping about in the shadows
    Not knowing what you should do?
Again, remember your Pilot,
    He knows the way that is right.
He will lead you, though you cannot see,
    Through the darkness into the light.

When your life on earth at last is done
    You will gaze at the glory bright
Of the heavenly city, your final home
    Where there will be no more night
For remember you have a Pilot
    Through tempests and dark times of life
Who will take you to that city
    Of eternal peace and light!

*L. Marie Enns*

# Of Crosses and Poppies

I traveled through a distant land
Where war was waged so long ago,
Explored a bunker chill and damp
That once hid soldiers from their foe.
I saw the craters gouged by shells,
The land made desolate by mines,
Memorials and a war museum,
Reminders all of awful times.

Along a forest path I walked
Where bits of twisted metal lay.
I heard a plane drone overhead,
An eerie token of that day
When planes meant bombs were hurtling down
And safety could not be assured
In field or forest nor in town,
And thousands fear and pain endured.

The path led to a field of grain
With dots of poppies sprinkled thin,
And then I saw beyond the field
A soldiers' graveyard stark and grim,
The silent voice of those now dead.
And mingled with the crosses white
The bravely swaying poppies red,
A sorrowful and silent sight.

And other graveyards, too, I saw
With, oh so many, rows of crosses,
So many, I was moved with awe
At the tremendous human losses.
As well, on concrete walls inscribed
Were lists and lists of those who died;
Too many names to comprehend,
And each one was some mother's pride.

O what a shame that humankind
Will hate and kill for greed and gain,
For power, glory, or for fame,
To cause such suffering, death and pain.
O Lord, cause all the wars to cease
Among the nations; guide their fate,
And help us all to live at peace,
To learn to love, and not to hate!

*L. Marie Enns*

# The Dieter's Lament

The sleeves are bulging in my dress. My bra is double rolled.
The calories I ate at lunch have multiplied untold!
My pantyhose are at half mast and cutting off my veins.
My extra fifty pounds or so are giving knee joint pains.

My waistline is herniated by the elastic in my dress
And as I speak, a button pops. (My own fault, I do confess.)
My underwear is crying out from definite overstrain.
My arches falling to my sole surely need a crane!

When waving bye to all my friends, my arm did slap my face.
I switched to slip on shoes this week, can't reach to tie a lace.
What is cause of this mutilation of body, heart and soul?
It's greed and self destruction. It's licking every bowl.

It's heartless condemnation of the real me, my goal.
It's eating, never thinking as I pile roll on roll.
If life is but three score and ten and I am halfway through it,
If thin is what I cherish, than I want to get me to it.

So this is me, my pain, my bod. Now is the time to start.
I'll throw aside my gluttony. From it I will depart.
I'll track what goes into my mouth and watch for sneaky bites.
Give up extra portions and butterscotch delights.

I'll put my tongue against my teeth and say n-n-n quite clearly,
Then form an 'O' with both my lips. There. I have it. Nearly.
No-No-No! That basic word that puts me on the path
To body slight and self-delight and no more poundly math.

And as my body slims away, on this you can depend.
That as I get me to it, on Christ I will depend.
Size twelve will own my closet and twenties disappear.
And I will face life gladly, even in the mirror.

*Brenda Wood*

# Racetrack Redemption

Karyn Wynalda-Booth

IT WAS A SUNDAY MORNING standing beside a sister in Christ, when the sludge settled on my soul. Although I did not know it at the time, I recall shifting my feet, shading my eyes in the bright light, uncomfortable with conviction creeping in. Before me the haze of swirling colours, undulating flags graceful in the shimmering heat mesmerized while earnest announcements begged my attention. My ears were deafened by the roaring growl, the idle of highly tuned machines, and I was transfixed. My heart beat faster, my breath caught, fists clenched, and soon it was over, the checker flag hailing the winner. The dust cloud enveloped again and I shuddered with the slowing cars returning to the pit. I watched the clearing vision ahead, soon tempered by a gentle spray, soothing the drying track. Choking back the settling dust, I was overcome by the heavy and undue judgment I had passed, but still unable to articulate what the foreboding feeling was about.

That morning found me in a most unlikely place, a sandy-coloured speedway where cars and drivers test their mettle. As one with a short and reluctant car ownership history, I giggled in astonishment at the plethora of cars when I stumbled out of the backseat as I joined friends to take up our place in the field. I wrinkled my nose, expecting dense fumes of exhaust, fuel, rubber, but the air was surprisingly clear and fresh. The competition was well underway, our sportsmen had been identified, and with each revolution, I felt less dissonance, and more goodwill, hope, approval.

I retreated to the shade, away from the action and realized how before me, was something so unexpected, an amazing and complex organism, a community. I had just seen a collection of diverse people working together, connected with a common purpose. Meeting regularly they displayed dedication to each other, themselves. Careful thought, intentional organization and schedule, concern and resources ready for the safety of all evident and ordinarily presented. Here, individuals arrived with creatively and carefully groomed and tuned entries, proud, but not above sharing a spare part, tool, or word of advice to someone stalled by an overlooked detail. The track was dominated by an air of respect coupled with a desire to perform well, to improve, maintained with the decorum of order.

Certainly the speedway has the same markers in community that I long for: diversity, enjoyment, improvement, creativity, and respect. Yet I had always chalked up my idea of community as something that I thought was, well, better, than say, car hobbies. My notion of an "ideal" community stemmed from schooling and a passion for ecology. I had proud and puffed-up visions of actual community, perhaps God ordained, as more organic, likely agrarian, lower technology. But here I was confronted with a car community that, on first quick and reluctant glance, was a well-oiled machine. I could not deny it. But I struggled to acknowledge that this scene was a generous and excellent example, because of its shameless dependence on fossil fuels.

The desire and need to invest time, energy, money, skill, and resources in a goal with others, a community, is something I share. I have cultivated and fertilized my mind to learning about the natural world, gardening, art, other cultures, music, and writing. I share the desire to do things enjoyable, to seek improvement, to do something well, with precision, grace. I seek a community of like-minded but diverse people, those who can meet with me, to share advice, tools, skill, and inspiration to continue my craft. I believe God has given me opportunity to pursue my passion, that He leads people into my path to help refine my pastime, and leads me to new books to read, or gardens to admire. And somehow in my own reverie, I had lost perspective.

Suddenly at the racetrack I saw someone like me. I was witnessing the sincere belief and dedication of one to this passion, coupled with the idea that God had some divine providence to pave the way for an individual to acquire and celebrate a novelty car. This blew my mind. I was silent and awestruck, suitably silenced in mind and heart knowing that God does give us the desires of our hearts, and sometimes, those are cars.

I am ill with humiliation at my arrogance, that I had cut God short of blessing another with this desire of heart, an auto hobby. My own hesitancy and reluctance to own a car was fuelled by my passionate environmental piety. Unable to escape the vice of fossil fuels, I ignored my indirect dependence through catching rides with others, "forgetting" my ownership of petroleum based products, and justifying borrowing other people's cars. I dared to forsake admiration of cars, but slipped furtive glances of awe deemed practically sinful to admit approval, for fear I would be validating them, and that would be anathema to my staunch environmental pride.

I began to see more clearly and painfully the large clod of dust in my own soul, and a new lingering strand of carsickness became apparent. I pulled off this track of thinking, and now sit in the infield while others continue the race. As I check things over, I want the referee to call me forward, to call me on my infraction, to reprimand me. I long for a yellow flag, to caution me, to get me back on track, a gentle and firm reminder to align my position, to stop passing judgment. I needed a gentle spray, a salve of forgiveness to cool my track of disrespect, and misunderstanding. Realistically, I have been careening out of control, deliberately and subversively bumping others with my snooty conceit, black flag criteria. I need to be pulled off the track, to acknowledge the danger of my thoughts, to plead for forgiveness. The sludge that had settled that morning was now a grateful realization that God expressed his creativity in forms much grander than I could know.

# *Angels Around Me*

Janet Seever

February 4, 2006, was a night like no other. I hadn't slept well for some reason, and at 3:30 a.m., just as I was drifting back to sleep, the light in our bedroom went on. A man was standing by our bed, glaring down at my husband and me. He had a short haircut and a goatee like our son Tim, who lives in our basement apartment, but when I got my eyes to focus, it definitely was not Tim. Barrel chested, the young man wore a black sweatshirt and two gold earrings.

"You're sleeping in my bed!" Anger rose in his voice. "You're living in my house! I've got papers to prove it."

It was no dream. This was real.

"Who are you?" I asked. "What's your name?"

He responded, "Ron."

I needed a phone, but it was in the kitchen. My husband woke up momentarily, but since he is handicapped from a stroke, he could do nothing to help. I had no way to contact my son in the basement. So it was just Ron and I as the drama unfolded.

"Let's go to the kitchen and talk about this," I said, getting out of bed and heading for the hall. I could tell Ron had been drinking because I could smell alcohol, although his speech wasn't slurred. Strangely enough, I was perfectly calm.

Still angry, Ron followed me to the kitchen.

"So this is your house?" I asked.

"Yes, I paid for it. But I suppose you need your sleep," he responded.

"If it's your house, would the police kick us out?"

He agreed they would.

"Shall I call them and see?" This was the opportunity I was looking for.

"It's 911," said Ron. He quit his tirade about owning the house and relaxed. When I asked him how he had gotten here, he said that the cab had dropped him off at the front door of "his house" and he had just walked in. Then I remembered—my husband had let in the cat before we went to bed, and I hadn't checked to see if he had relocked the door.

So I called 911. I calmly explained to the woman at the other end that I had a man in my kitchen, who said he owned the house we were living in. She transferred me to the police department.

During our conversation, the police dispatcher said, "You sound calm," to which I agreed and said Ron wasn't threatening me, he just wanted his house back. (I hoped she didn't think I was too calm and dismiss this as a prank call.)

Ron was completely cooperative, answering questions about himself for the police dispatcher on the other end of the line as I relayed the questions to him– he was 5'10", 300 pounds (I think he was mistaken about that), 27 years old, dressed in a black shirt and sweatshirt. He then rolled up his sleeve to show me he had a tattoo. He also gave us his full name this time.

Shortly afterward, we heard the door open—it was still unlocked. Two police officers entered.

"Do you still think you own this house?" they asked Ron as he walked toward the door. At this point he had sobered up enough to agree that the house didn't look anything like his, and he gave them his address in the next subdivision.

"I've never seen this woman before in my life," he said, referring to me. He apologized profusely for entering our house by mistake.

In thinking about the incident afterward, I reflected on the fact that I never felt terrified. Part of the reason was that I had been in difficult situations previously with irrational people and had talked my way through them. I knew what to do.

But I said it was just Ron and I. That's not really true. I think God had His angels encamped around me. And getting Ron to agree to my phoning the police? I don't normally think that clearly in the middle of the night, especially in stressful situations.

I think God gave me the words to say.

# *Heavenly Food*

Elsie Montgomery

My daughter cannot eat bread. She isn't celiac but has a problem with gluten. I cannot imagine going without bread, even though Jesus said that I do not live by bread alone.… I think that I could, or at least I did.

Lately I've not been eating regular bread, only the sprouted grain variety. Yesterday I had some regular bread and my tummy didn't like it. I'm glad this is not true of all bread, especially when I read this verse from my devotional book this morning.

"I am the living bread which came down from heaven. If anyone eats of this bread, he will live forever; and the bread that I shall give is My flesh, which I shall give for the life of the world" (John 6:51 NKJV).

Jesus talked to a crowd that chased after Him when they heard He had multiplied a few loaves of bread into enough to feed thousands. However, He knew why they were there. He said, "Most assuredly, I say to you, you seek Me, not because you saw the signs, but because you ate of the loaves and were filled. Do not labor for the food which perishes, but for the food which endures to everlasting life, which the Son of Man will give you, because God the Father has set His seal on Him." (John 6:26–27 NKJV)

They didn't get it, but He kept talking. He told them that

He was the living bread, the source of eternal life, but they had to eat this bread to have that life. They still didn't get it.

Neither did His disciples. After the crowd was gone, they asked Jesus about this "hard saying." In part, He told them, "It is the Spirit who gives life; the flesh profits nothing. The words that I speak to you are spirit, and they are life." (John 6:63 NKJV)

Since I became a Christian, I've looked at many different views about Jesus. Almost all of them have no idea what it means to "eat" the flesh of Jesus. Some think it is a symbol. Some think it is a horrible cannibalism. Without the enlightening power of the Holy Spirit, I agree that this is a strange and hard saying. Yet God explains the key to understanding Jesus' words through the words of Paul:

"These things we also speak, not in words which man's wisdom teaches but which the Holy Spirit teaches, comparing spiritual things with spiritual. But the natural man does not receive the things of the Spirit of God, for they are foolishness to him; nor can he know them, because they are spiritually discerned" (1 Corinthians 2:13–14 NKJV)

Without the Holy Spirit, no one can fully understand the Bible. Even with the Holy Spirit, Christians get truth "here a little, there a little" for that is the way of God. He knows what I need to know. He does not give me all of it at once. To do so would be like trying to eat a bakery full of bread. My body could not tolerate it. Instead, God gives me a small slice at a time, just what I need. In the beginning, my first taste of Jesus meant that He gave me Himself. In doing so, He now lives in me and I have eternal life.

Since that day, the Spirit has fed me many things. For instance, Jesus is the Word of God, the living Word for sure, but also the written Word. It is this Word that I feast on, reading, chewing, digesting — knowing, remembering, understanding, obeying. By doing this, I am feasting on Christ. He becomes my spiritual nourishment and sustenance. Without a proper spiritual diet, my spiritual life would weaken into uselessness.

Using the same 'bread' analogy, Jesus said, "Man shall not live by bread alone, but by every word that proceeds from the mouth of God." (Matthew 4:4 NKJV)

In this verse, the Greek term translated "word" is rhema. It means "that which is needed for the moment." In other words, God gives me the portion that I need for each day, my "daily bread." I cannot gorge myself. He controls the portions because He knows me as His created and adopted child and knows what I need to be strong and live for Him.

I marvel at the wonderful care of God. He gave me spiritual life in Christ then feeds that life by drawing me into His Word and near to Him. No banquet could taste better or be more important that sitting down to a meal with Jesus.

# *Jars of Clay*

Robert White

POTTERY IS AN APT METAPHOR FOR God's work.

After a friend of mine took over a pottery business a few years ago, my family and I decided to spend a morning "pot-ter"ing around.

No matter how many times I watch a potter take a lump of clay, form and fire it into something beautiful, the process still fascinates me. In this case, family members were working on bisque pieces: a goblet, a frog and a heart. And, while I may be able to paint a pretty picture with words, the actual act of painting on clay that's been molded, dried, cleaned and fired is beyond my capabilities. I'd gladly watch, in awe, those whose talent turned the plain pieces of white clay into beautiful pieces of art.

What fascinated me this time around was the actual process of painting. My son, who decided to paint his goblet black, expressed some dismay when, after a third coat of paint, the goblet looked more a dull gray color than the shiny black on the sample piece of clay. Only after the glazing and a final firing in a nearly 2,000 degree kiln for about 48 to 72 hours, did the sheen show up.

It's no wonder the apostle Paul used the pottery image twice in his writings.

In Romans, Paul was responding to those who wanted to question why God chose one person for one task and another person for another task, instead of vice versa. "Do you for one moment suppose any of us knows enough to call God into question?…Isn't it obvious that a potter has a perfect right to shape one lump of clay into a vase for holding flowers and another into a pot for cooking beans?" writes Paul (Romans 9:20, 21, *The Message*).

To the Christians in Corinth, Paul focused on how people miss the most obvious because it's wrapped up in a plain package: "We carry this precious Message around in the unadorned clay pots of our ordinary lives" (2 Corinthians 4:7 *The Message*). But, he continues, "That's to prevent anyone from confusing God's incomparable power with us."

As a raw product, clay can be extremely flexible—able to be molded into practically any shape the potter desires. And, usually, until the final firing, it is drab and unattractive. As I look at my own life in the hands of the Master Potter, I need to ask: am I flexible? Or do I, as Paul suggests, call God into question because I don't like the shape I'm taking.

Or do I want a showier glaze so that people see me and my efforts, rather than the "incomparable power" of God shining through me? Am I content to be a plain jar of clay?

While it shouldn't surprise me, once again, God used the imagery of pottery—the plain bisque, the drab colors of an unfired painted piece—to teach me a lesson: it's only in the hands of the Master Potter a lump of clay can become a work of art.

# "Girl, I Lost You"

Bonnie Way

WHEN I FINALLY HAD WHAT I'D wanted for so long, my first emotion was bitterness. My manager clapped my back, my drummer and guitarist grinned like Cheshire cats, and the lighting tech gave me a thumbs-up while the screams of the crowd still echoed over the stage. I tried to grin, to act as excited as they were over the best concert I'd done since "Girl, I Lost You" hit the top twenty charts, but all I could think was that she wasn't there.

"They're lovin' it." Jerry pulled me down the hallway toward the dressing room. "Look, you got twenty minutes to catch a drink and clean up, then we got the after-concert party. And Eric—"

He jerked me around in front of the door and peered up at me. For a minute, I thought he'd catch the way I pined for the one person whose congratulations I wasn't getting.

"I know you're exhausted, but ratings and sales depend upon the fans. This party is crucial. So have a coffee, a Big Mac, do what you gotta do, but put on a good face in twenty, got it?"

He never noticed my grin only stretched my lips. "Yeah, man. Thanks."

He was halfway down the hallway before I opened the dressing room door. I knew he'd be cracking his knuckles, congratulating himself on the concert, taking the credit for making me a top country star. Well, he'd been a big part—but she'd been a bigger part.

I dropped into the lopsided chair and pressed my forehead into my palms. How many years had I been working toward this day? Eight in Nashville, but it had begun long before that, when I'd been a teenage boy strumming my guitar and penning my own lyrics. Sure, those first attempts had been cheesy, but Claire hadn't cared.

I smiled at the memory of her singing along with the first song I recorded on my tape player. She sang off-key. Always did, no matter how many times I coached her. She'd just laugh and say singing was my department; she'd be the woman behind the great man. Except she wasn't.

Had she even heard my latest song? Maybe she listened to rock music now. Maybe she was hiding in Nunavut or some place with no radio. No way for memories of me to interrupt her new life. Maybe she'd found someone else.

I lunged across the room to peer into the mirror. I dragged a comb through my hair, letting the teeth dig into my scalp, as if pain there could compensate for pain in my heart. Smile, I thought, practicing my I'm-glad-you-like-my-music smile. Claire would say I looked like a jackass.

A fist banging on the door brought me around with a jerk. Jerry didn't wait for me to open it.

"It's not a Big Mac, but it'll have to do." He handed me a paper bag. "Remember to brush your teeth. I had one star who gagged all his fans with bad breath."

"Minty fresh," I promised, ripping the burger out of its wrapping. "Say, the party… anybody I know there?"

He rolled his eyes upwards. "Nope. 'Least nobody I know. You expecting anyone?"

I shrugged, pretending it didn't matter. He'd known Claire in Nashville, so he'd remember her. "Just thought maybe someone would show up, since my hometown is forty minutes away."

"Yeah. Probably the neighbour's snotty-nosed kid." He punched my shoulder and scooted toward the door. "See you there."

"Yep," I said to the closed door, and finished the burger. I washed my face, brushed my teeth, combed my hair again, and checked the clock. Ten minutes. Never appear early, Jerry said. I dropped onto the chair and rested my head on my arms.

She wasn't coming. All these months I'd waited for this stop on the tour. Hoped somehow she'd get a ticket, come backstage, and now… she wasn't here.

I tugged the chain out from under my shirt and peered at the ring. It looked tiny in my fingers, like I'd snap the band and lose the diamond, but on her hand, it was perfect. I knew it was meant for her when I first saw it. Carried it around with me for a month before I proposed, just before I signed the record deal and she joined me in Nashville. Now I carried it around again, wondering if I'd ever get it back onto her hand.

Was there anything I could have said on that night to change her mind? Maybe if I'd ignored the phone, told Jerry that the biggest bar in the world could ask for me but I wasn't coming because I was with Claire, found some way to tell her she was number one in my life…

Except she hadn't been. The music had taken over. Obsessed me. Fame, fortune, and all that. How long had she waited, tried to win me back? I couldn't imagine. Even the pain of her leaving hadn't hit me until months after. I had my music. And I was angry.

I tucked the ring back into my shirt and closed my eyes. "Girl, I Lost You" was my last hope to find her. It was my apology. I wrote it for her, not for the fans. I never meant it to be a hit, but the only way for her to hear it was to release it for radio. She'd moved away, wouldn't answer my emails, changed her cell number. I couldn't find her. Except through my music.

Maybe I was a fool to think the thing that had pushed her away could bring her back. But it was all I had.

The door clicked behind me. I tensed, wondering what Jerry wanted now. It was probably time to smile at those fans and pretend life as the big country singer was great. I drew in a breath and started to turn, but a soft voice stopped me.

"Eric."

# For God So Loved

Abandoned Savior
bruised and beaten,
stumbling on the cobblestone…
weighted with the cross of Calvary,
in a crowd, yet all alone.

Broken Savior
hanging helpless,
callous hearts watch as You bleed…
oozing gashes, aching, throbbing,
victim of deceit and greed.

Abused Savior
crowned in satire,
thorns like talons pierce Your brow…
closest comrades, those You trusted
now Your friendship disavow.

Lifeless Savior
pain has ended,
head is pendant on Your chest…
hands that healed lay mutilated.
You, for me, endured this test?

Loving Savior
full of mercy,
suffering for the human race…
patient, kind, forgiving Master,
I embrace Your gift of grace!

Living Savior
You have risen!
death is swallowed in defeat…
battle fought, triumphant victory!
sin is conquered.
Plan complete!

*Geraldine Nicholas*

# the smell of rain

the smell of rain is the smell of earth
the dark rich
yields pungent secrets
bits of life in your nostrils
stolen aromas of spruce sap and black willow bark

soaking life-giving event
listen to it river dance on the roof
kick heels against the window pane
to the clapping rhythm of the trees

let the raindrops run down your face
drip from your eyebrows

let them wash away the cobwebs of inertia
plant seeds of angels in your brain

when the yellow finch flits
near raindrops
dangling on purple columbines
let the chorus of bird songs fill your ears
as the smell of the earth
sends forth praise from your lips
rising to heaven
like the smell of new rain

*Linda Siebenga*

# Passion Play in Drumheller Badlands

rugged convoluted Drumheller hills
where badlands echo the irregular crow of the cock
bleat of goats and sheep shepherded in the distance
beyond a noisy street  peopled with Mary Martha
disciples    Pharisees    and children    not unfamiliar people

fishing boat by the wharf  in our ears the shofar horn
in our noses the acrid smell of burning altar fire

our bodies swayed by the Jewish wedding music
accompanying the procession through the streets

our seats located too close to Your shudder
as the spikes crunch through Your carpenter hands
too close to the smell of the wood rough
against Your tattered bleeding back

perhaps it was the music and You dancing
that twigged a sense of joy     the small children
in Your arms    held close and cherished

perhaps it was the pleasure of Mary's delight
on seeing You after Your resurrection

or the succulent melon You broke open
fruit of the vine in hands that were broken for me

how You rode home in the car with us
some anachronism after the donkey scene

and how You hold our grandchildren so tenderly
bless our baked potatoes and share our poignant moments

*Linda Siebenga*

# The Calligraphy of Your Love

Your name is written
　　on everything around us

the deck frames overflow
　　with the calligraphy of your love
furniture fashioned from your diamond willows
　　bent into lines of comfort
round cushions made of cotton
　　that grew in the heat of your sun
curlicues of prim parsley
　　tucked under the tangled lines
　　　　of tomato vines in the bushel basket
the smell of apple blossoms and lilacs
　　　　curling under our noses

if I would recognize your name
　　　　on every square inch of my life
each breakfast prayer would celebrate
　　the roundness of the bursting blueberry you fashioned
　　　　perched on crinkled flakes of your corn
　　splashed with smooth streaming lines of designer milk

each bite of bold whole wheat toast
　　　　with subtle strokes of honey
　　would be a remembrance of your care
　　　　a gift of your hand written into my life

*Linda Siebenga*

# A Farm Kid's Playground

Sheri Hathaway

I HAD JUST CHOPPED DOWN another slim poplar and James was cutting it into pieces while I rested. I sat on the prickly grass cross-legged, my red hands laid palms up on my lap so the warm sun and cool breeze could work their comforting salve on them. I watched the bees and dragonflies. The clear, pungent fragrance of freshly cut poplar added to the cleanness of the air. How I loved that smell! The sun warmed everything in its sight, smiling down on the grass and trees with its blessings. As if singing a song with the sun, the breeze smoothed over the places where too much heat had settled, cooling all to perfect harmony. A crow sailed overhead, mocking the stillness with his raucous insults. Busy sparrows in the branches over our heads twittered secretively together as they went about their business. Far away a meadowlark exploded with joy. We talked quietly as we worked. There was no need for louder voices in this peaceful spot in the pasture. The poplars laughed low in whispery voices, their leaves twirling like copper pennies on strings. The water in the beaver dam rippled a low murmuring and, look, there was the duck family out again, dabbling busily after water bugs and prattling to each other in their funny, croaky voices. Once we saw a whole family of toads on their bumpy journey to new homes. We stopped our work to watch the parade, advancing like so many undisciplined soldiers. The pasture was our private playground where we spent many a summer day exploring or playing. We enjoyed the nature around us as much as we reveled in the adventures we had. Occasionally the cows lumbered past us, but they were used to us, and we ignored them as city kids might ignore the cranky neighbor lady passing by.

On this day, we were into the second week of building our fort. It consisted of a lean-to of slim poplar trunks that rested from the ground up to a larger tree which had blown over during a high wind and was clutched in the topmost arms of its neighbor. We had found it on one of our walks in quest for adventure and decided right then and there what we would do. James ran home to get the hatchet, hammer and nails. We knew our parents wouldn't approve of us having the tools, especially the hatchet. Each day we snuck them out of the shop when no one was around. When we had built enough of a shelter to hide them, we got bold enough to leave them out there.

Although we were very proud of our accomplishment, we were also finding out the costs of our labor. Blisters stood out on our hands from gripping the tools hard enough to make them work. Our backs and arms ached, especially from the chopping. The hatchet probably was not very sharp and we had to swing it with all the strength that our ten and eleven-year-old arms could muster. When we had enough poles attached for one of us to lay down and put our head in, we saw that it needed clay to fill the gaps. The bumpy, twisty poplars made large holes when we fitted them together – some big enough for our hands to fit through. The clay scooped easily from the banks of the dam. Its cool smoothness felt good on our burning palms and this type of work became our favorite over the chopping.

We enjoyed the work more than the product. We loved the warm quiet of the spot next to the dam, sheltered by the poplar bush and we had a purpose for our labor. We were building a fort and it was the building of it, among nature's people, that was our pleasure. When it was done, at least as much as our hands and arms would allow, we lost interest in it. We were past the days of pretending to be cowboys in the Old West and anyway, our attention had turned elsewhere by then. On other exploits in the pasture after that, we sometimes came across our old fort and always took a good look, noticing how the weather and time was claiming it back, and remembering those warm and pleasant days when we built it.

# *My Heritage*

Elaine Ingalls Hogg

All day I had sorted through old newspaper clippings. Most of the people in the clippings were just names, but the yellowed church envelope I held in my hand triggered a memory. I saw her in my mind, sitting by the kitchen window in her small Wood Island home. When I first met her she was already an old woman, ninety years old and I was but a child. More than fifty years have passed since the day she died, Sarah, Sarah Maude Shepherd, my great grandmother. Slowly I turned the envelope over and read the words she penned there.

*TO MY CHILDREN*

*I leave this old book as the best heritage I can give. Study it carefully and you will find the way to peace and righteousness and happiness as I have done. If there is ever anything wrong with your lives, come back to this book as if it were a looking glass and it will clearly show you what is the matter. And when you are lost in the world it will guide you home. MOTHER*

I want to know about you Sarah. I want to trace the ties that are still reaching down through the years and drawing me back to my roots; to meet the women who raised sons to go out on the sea, to go to war and not come home and learn of the men who toiled long and hard battling the elements yet took time to wipe away their child's tears.

Shortly after I found the clipping I learned of a family reunion where the Wood Island families gathered to tell their stories. I decided to make the trip.

After a six-hour car trip I found myself waiting for the boat. There was already a line up. I counted the cars ahead of me. If I made this boat I would be home in two more hours! I got out of the car so I could smell the salt air, watch the fishing boats moving to and fro, listen to the pounding surf and the call of the gulls. The wait was good; it allowed me time to prepare for the slower island pace. The boat drew into dock and the attendant beckoned me to go aboard. I made it. I was the last car on.

The next morning Dad and I found a few minutes together and I asked him to tell me once again the story of how he learned to play the violin. When he was a teenager, he discovered an old violin in the attic of the family homestead. Although there was no violin teacher in the area, he studied a US School of Music Correspondence Course he found in the attic. Dad still plays his music daily. It amazes me that a ninety-one year old man can bring such a marvellous sound from his instrument. I'm sure I inherited my love of music from my dad.

Later I went to visit dad's brother. He told me stories—stories of my people, of fishing, and about his first car. My grandfather took the car for a drive one day and when he was returning home he forgot how to use the brakes. When he finally parked, the back end of the garage was opened to the world and the steering wheel was in his lap. But the best thing I remember about my visit was how my uncle, who up until now was a reserved, stalwart fisherman not given to showing his emotions, gave me a hug and a kiss. Thank you Uncle Hart, you've reminded me how important it is to give our hugs and kisses while we are still living.

Friday evening the Wood Island families gathered at the community hall to meet and greet one another. There were pictures on the wall and old photo albums to look through, people to see and the old refrains to hear,

*"Who's your great, great, great grandfather? Or 'What brings you back? "My roots, everything, my whole heritage."* My cousin's answer made me realise some of my own reasons for making this journey.

Great Aunt Lila reminded me of my great grandmother's faith. How after all the work was done and the children were put in bed, Sarah Maude would kneel at a chair in the corner on the family dog, Mike's, mat. Here she would pray for each member of her family. Godliness was important to my ansestors.

Saturday afternoon the young and old alike gathered at the Seal Cove wharf where they waited to climb aboard the fishing boat; the *Island Bound* which took us over to Wood Island for the family picnic. The sun danced on the water, people chatted together, memories and stories began. "Here's where we played on the rocks," my mother said. "The long rocks became our dolls and we dressed them in mermaid silk."

"Over there we made clay dishes," Annie added. "And we made paper dolls out of catalogues." Listening to them, I recognised the ability to amuse myself by using my imagination is part of my heritage.

On a warm Sunday afternoon I joined my relatives who gathered for an afternoon service in the small white church that stands like a monument to the people who once lived on Wood Island. At first I was disappointed when I took the path leading from the beach to the church. Except for one older home and a couple of cabins, the island looked abandoned. It reminded me of the fluff from a dandelion. Only a faint outline remained.

I sang the old hymns, *Amazing Grace, In My Heart there Rings a Melody* but when we sang *Let the Lower Lights Be*

*Burning*, I knew I had discovered what this island really means to me. My ancestors' faith was still reaching down through the generations and lighting the way for me, for my children and my grandchildren. What a heritage!

# Slowest Mammal on Earth

Violet Nesdoly

THE JUNGLE IS STILL. BUT WAIT. Out of the corner of your eye – movement. You look up and see a brownish-green creature descending a tree – slowly but steadily, limb to limb. When it reaches the forest floor this housecat-sized animal loses its grace. It digs into the earth with its front claws and pulls itself along on its belly, dragging its hind legs. At a certain spot it stops and takes a bathroom break. Then it struggles back to its tree, reaches for the lowest limb and, branch to branch, ascends again to the leafy canopy.

You have just seen a sloth take his once-a-week trip to the bathroom – a spot on the ground that he uses over and over. These South and Central American mammals spend most of their lives hanging upside down from tree branches in the jungle. There they sleep for ten to fifteen hours a day, eat, mate and have their babies. They only come to the ground to get rid of waste or change trees. And they do everything very, very slowly. They are famous for being the slowest mammals on earth. Even when in danger, they move only fifteen feet (about the length of a pickup truck) per minute – a distance you could walk in a few seconds.

Sloths were first called *pregucia* –Portuguese for sloth—by explorers in the 1600s. The word *sloth* comes from the old English word *slowth*. It means inaction, slowness, laziness, sluggishness, lethargy, and loafing.

But sloths are not really lazy. God made them slow to survive in their jungle home. Sloths eat mostly leaves, shoots, and fruit. Their diet doesn't provide many calories and is hard to digest. It can take up to a month for their complex stomachs to completely break down food. Their slow life and low muscle mass helps them conserve energy. Their low body temperature does too. It ranges between 86 to 93F when they are active and even lower when they sleep. By comparison, your body must stay within about two thirds of a degree (0.6F) of 98.2F for you to feel well.

You may wonder how such slow-moving animal survives in a jungle full of fierce and quick-moving enemies. Even for this it is well suited. A sloth's gray, brown or tan fur slants away from its stomach. This makes the rain shed off its upside-down body and allows it to stay in the treetops even in wet weather. Because it stays so still, its fur grows green algae. This camouflages it as it hangs amongst the leaves. Its ability to stay still keeps its presence a secret from sharp-eyed predators like the harpy eagle and the jaguar, who detect prey by movement. The sloth is also nocturnal. It is most active at night when the forest is dark and sleeps during the daytime.

If you're in the middle of chores, assignments, tests and work, a sloth's life of sleeping all day may seem pretty attractive. But don't be tempted to copy the sloth. As a human you're made differently. If you eat good food you'll have the energy you need. Plenty of exercise will help you develop well-toned muscles that enable you to move slowly and quickly. God also gave you a mind that can calculate, imagine, invent, create, and plan. So live wisely and heed the Bible's warning against the natural human tendency toward laziness. Because slothfulness in people doesn't lead to an idyllic jungle existence but to poverty, hunger and a messy home (Proverbs 6:11; 10:2-5; 24:30-31).

In the meantime, visit the sloths next time you're at the zoo. As you watch them sleep, chew leaves, or inch from branch to branch, thank God for the variety of His wonderful creation that includes both sloths and you.

# *En Plein Air*

Carmen Wise

*"Come, my dear. Take my hand, be with me."*

THE VOICE NEARLY JOLTED LIDIA off her bench. She had heard someone speak. She looked around. There was no one else in the room. The young security guard was perched on a stool out in the hall.

Lidia turned her attention back to the massive painting that covered the whole wall. It was one of Monet's earlier creations entitled *Dejeuner Sur l'Herbe.* It depicted a picnic with friends gathered in a grassy spot in a verdant forest. Some sat on a food-laden blanket spread out on the ground. Others stood or walked about. The women were resplendent in gold, silver, and frothy white gowns, the gentlemen debonair and elegant in fine black morning coats and top hats. But for one young man who, with an "air of insouciance" had tossed his coat aside and stretched out his lanky frame half on the picnic blanket, half on the grass.

Lidia Carlson, 77, had been an artist herself. She loved coming to the French Impressionism Gallery of the Museum of Art. She had found herself lingering more and more before the great painting by Monet. The artist's use of light and dark on the canvas fascinated her. Otherwise dark and austere, the canvas came to life with the painter's judicious spattering of sun light. In deeper parts of the forest where the shadows were licked by the sun's rays, colors shifted from a deep hunter green, almost black, to emerald, then to chartreuse. Leaves seemed to shiver with a light of their own. The picnic scene came alive, seemingly touched by a whisper of wind that nudged leaves and caused tall blades of grass to sway delicately. Even the boughs of branches, laden with tiny flowers, dipped and lifted.

*"Bonjour, Mademoiselle. Voulez vous nous joindre?" (Hello Miss. Would you like to join us?)*

Again, the voice. She looked for its source. Then she caught a movement in the painting. The bearded young man on the grass was sitting upright, looking directly at her.

"Mrs. Carlson." The security guard's voice startled her.

"Oh, hello. Sarah, isn't it?" she asked.

"Yes, ma'am. I just wanted to let you know it's closing time in a few minutes."

"Already? I must have dozed off." She pushed herself up with her cane. "Sarah, in the painting, that young man, there, doesn't he appear a little different? "

Sarah followed her pointing finger. "I'm sorry, Mrs. Carlson. I don't know the painting well enough. Why, do you think someone touched it?"

"Oh, no. No. I guess my imagination is getting the best of me," Lidia answered. "See you tomorrow, Sarah." Lidia walked to the elevator.

On the elderly lady's next visit, Sarah asked Mrs. Carlson, "I was wondering, ma'am, what you like so much about that painting? It's so different from the hazy ones you think of when you think of Monet."

Lidia smiled. "It reminds me of my youth in France, going on picnics, parties, outings. I look at it and suddenly I'm there, enjoying the fresh air and camaraderie. Monet preferred to paint outdoors, 'en plein air' he called it. He would say he wanted to catch an 'impression' of a scene before him. In this way he could satisfy the observer's senses, incite an emotional response, and excite the imagination."

The next day Mrs. Carlson showed Sarah a small black and white photo encased in a small silver frame.

"A lifetime ago, I visited Monet's homestead just outside Giverny," she explained. "I stood on the little bridge overlooking his Lily Pond. I watched my reflection on the glassy water. Another reflection nudged mine. It belonged to Paul, the man who would become my husband. There were flowers everywhere, pretty, like those pastel gossamer dresses." Lidia looked at the painting.

"Paul passed on twenty years ago," Lidia continued.

Sarah looked at the photograph. "Why, you were such a lovely couple," she noted. She looked at it closely. "Mrs. Carlson, have you noticed how much that guy in the painting resembles your husband?" she asked.

Lidia looked down. "Oh. Maybe so." She carefully tucked the frame into her purse. She then untied her beautiful silk scarf.

"This is a Hermes scarf." She reached up to wrap it around Sarah's neck. "Paul gave it to me on our first anniversary. Look, it brings roses to your cheeks."

"Oh, Mrs. Carlson, I can't take this. It means too much to you."

"Nothing would make happier that to see a lovely young lady enjoy it for the rest of her life. As I did."

A group of school children clamored their way into the gallery. Sarah excused herself to watch over them.

Lidia returned to her study of the Monet painting. Again movement caught her eye.

*"Bonjour Mademoiselle. Etes vous triste?" (Hello Miss. Are you sad?)*

In some unfathomable way, the young man in the painting

was talking to her.

*"Pas du tout," she laughed. "En fait je me sens animee, contente, si meilleure depuis quelques ans. " (Not at all. In fact, I feel happier, content, so much better than I have in years.)*

He held his hand out to her. *"L'air c'est douce, comme une caresse, une baisse." (The breeze is sweet, like a caress, or a kiss. )"Ca done la Sante." (This brings good health).* Lidia's hand fluttered to his grasp like a tiny bird.

Sarah returned to the Gallery a few minutes later. To her surprise, Mrs. Carlson was not in her usual spot. On the bench lay the framed picture of Paul and Lidia. As she went to pick up the photo, Sarah looked at the painting. Was she imagining things or was there a new person in the painting? Yes, another young woman. She was smiling at the lanky young gentleman who held her hand to his lips.

Sarah tightened the silk scarf around her neck and walked back to her stool.

# The Other Side (An Allegory)

Janice L. Dick

THE FIRES ENCIRCLING THE Plateau blaze unacknowledged by its inhabitants. Strangers from The Valley and Beyond have migrated here to escape the heat, but none recognize the creeping flames. Buyers and sellers continue to ply their trade, heedless of the influx of Foreigners who trample their wares underfoot as they come.

As the camps of The People drift away from the flames, Erda packs up her clay pots and kiln, and relocates. A dark red scarf covers her mouth and nose against the acrid smoke hanging in the air. She does not turn to look, but blows soot off her newly fired pots and reaches for another chunk of clay.

Fairlie and Disa see the fires. "Come with us to The Other Side," they plead. "There is still time to escape."

The fires advance slowly and steadily, growing higher and hotter. The People of The Land gather nearer The Chasm, some exhibiting courage to peek over the edge, displaying no sign that they hear wailing and grinding from below, or see smoke wisps ascending on torrid air currents.

Fairlie and Disa, clothed in masks and cloaks, slip through the crowds in the direction of The Bridge. As they struggle against the jostling horde, they call out, "Come with us. The Gate is still open." They are, for the most part, ignored. Erda hears but does not respond. The Remnant, as the two are called, step through The Gate and onto the Bridge, shedding their protective gear.

The People of the Plateau are familiar with The Bridge. It has always connected the two sides of The Chasm, as long as any of them can remember. Foreigners have also been told of its existence, but it is not well-traveled. In fact, it is spoken of derisively, if it is spoken of at all.

Perhaps one reason is that the People do not know for sure what is on The Other Side: preparations for some kind of celebration, according to Fairlie and Disa. No one has ever returned from there to confirm it.

At one point in the history of The Land, there was said to be One Individual who claimed to be from The Other Side. But who is to know? And now that is merely words on the pages of some ancient manuscript.

At times, when their senses are keen, The People of the Plateau hear Almost-Laughter rippling over the air waves from The Other Side. During brief spells when their eyes are in focus and air pollution is minimal, they behold a peculiar shimmering of Almost-Colors rising from That Place.

But That Place is not the concern of the Plateau Dwellers. They have long ago declared themselves an independent society. To be free, in The Edict of The People, is to be "independent of any ties or responsibilities that limit the moment-to-moment choices of an individual."

Crossing of The Bridge is not encouraged—it implies weakness. Besides, would one ever get back to The Plateau if he or she did not like it on The Other Side, or if The Other Side were simply an illusion?

The embers that have smoldered on the outer boundaries of The Land for centuries with increasing determination have become roaring flames and exploding gases. Thunderous blasts rock the now-crackling atmosphere. The People edge closer and closer to The Chasm.

Daegel, seller of scarves, stands with the rest of his people. A spark from the inferno settles on his shoulder and he turns. Red-orange flames meet his gaze.

"Help me!" he cries out, "I'm coming across." But The Remnant has since stepped onto The Bridge and they do not look back. The crowds push the agonized Daegel back toward the flames, crushing him.

"We are free to decline the crossing of The Bridge," they chant through soot-blackened gauze, eyes streaming from the smoke.

Another of The People, Mellis the gold-merchant, nears the brink of The Chasm with resolute step, as if to catch a whiff of sulfur, and in that instant, dives onto The Bridge. The Gate clangs shut behind him as The People crowd its solid steel door, chanting, "Freedom to deny, freedom to decline."

They have never seen The Gate closed before. From farther along The Chasm, they see that The Bridge has also been withdrawn.

Odd whimpers are heard among the crowds of The People now. Snivelers are tossed into The Chasm, their screams blocked by chanting. Laughter begins as a cover, then transforms into a unifying force, building in ever-increasing crescendo to a fearsome howl. A distant din from The Chasm rises in terrifying harmony.

Suddenly, at the silver blaring of trumpets from Above and Around, the noise ceases. Deafening silence reigns.

Faint shimmering colors rise above The Chasm and float near The Plateau. A Great Glorious Light appears, holding The People entranced. They drop to their knees as their legs give way. Erda's clay pots crash to the dirt; her hands come up to cover her face. From drooping jaws and with one accord, The People hail The Eminence.

In uncanny organization, they proceed, one by one, to approach The Blinding Light, to the very edge of The Chasm.

Erda stumbles forward as if her legs are not her own. But as she and the others approach, The Eminence does not recognize them and they do not reach out to It, so they slip over the brink with voiceless screams, and do not cease from falling.

When the entire population of The Plateau, including Foreigners from The Valley and Beyond, has been dispatched, their entire Dwelling Place erupts in a burst of ash and dirt and smoke, and disappears into The Chasm.

Then from across The Expanse, from where The Glory emanates, wafts the sound of celebration, singing and dancing and joyful adoration of True Freedom in the Light. And the Party goes on forever.

The End

(of the beginning)

Jeremiah 4:11- 5:18 and Revelation 21:18 - 22:5

# Mountains

In the desert prepare the way for the Lord;
Make straight in the wilderness a highway for our God …
Every mountain and hill [shall be] made low
The rough ground shall become level (Is. 40:3,4 NIV).
You who bring good tidings to Zion
Go up on a high mountain (Is. 40:9 NIV).

The country would have beautiful scenery
if every time you wanted to see
there wasn't a mountain
blocking your view
but every mountain and hill
which might impede the view to my God
shall be levelled

My every mountain and hill
every impediment and detour
shall be levelled
to make a straight path
a highway for our God
a highway to my God
a highway

Every step upward seems a hill
every incline a wall
every cliff a fortress
every hill a mountain
every summit insurmountable

but every mountain and hill
shall be made low
and the glory of the Lord
shall be revealed

Every mountain and hill
shall be made low
except those we shall leave
to climb and shout the good tidings
to Zion the city of our God

*Alvin G. Ens*

# For Dianne

Now you see no shadows
    feel no rain
    nor see sunshafts
        part the clouds
like smiles that light young faces
    at the bell

And now the children's voices fade
    to echoes hovering
    'round the mound that hides
        you from this world

No gilded monument rises to proclaim your work
    Yet there is this:
        the light of learning –
            the gift that lives
            for time to come –
        still glows within the hearts of those
            who passed your way

And what of us, and what we shared?

We live not where the ground
    is overturned
        and you are laid to rest
There are miles – and more
    much more
        between us now

where once we touched
    through work and sometimes
        play

And yet we have your wit
    the raspy laugh that cut
    through pretense like a blade
        Who could forget?

We know the way you strove
    to give your best
And value how you understood
    the complexities of learning
We celebrate those brief few minutes of your life
    we were privileged to share

And let us say this much:
    that we will not forget
        — though years pass by —
    the intersecting of our lives
        and that we are better for it

If we could give these words
    the power
        to pull you back
    we would but no
            we know
    it can't be done
And there is but this sad point —
    that you were one of us, Dianne
        and now
            are gone — too soon

*Hugh Smith*

# mortality

i smell
that wispy curl
wasping
over your finger tips
like grey
cat's tail
enveloping your beauty
a spirit going free

you struggle with
this dark load
you need not carry alone

he'll bridge your world
and the world
beyond
do you understand –
from here within
this purpled span?

mortality
    i have a nose for it
but love to touch
    that greater love
        beyond
who seals synaptic affection
    with a touch
        transcending
    mere epidermal charge

i bury my face in your soft grey sweater

*Hugh Smith*

# Tentacles of Night (song lyrics)

For you a bloodshot sun dispels the night,
It peels off a dark and filthy cloak.
You owned the night, all wreathed in musk and smoke;
Today your naked shame lies quivering in the light.

Do eternal whispers draw you any longer,
Or has your hope been long since shut away?
You suffer through another endless day,
And the tentacles of night grow ever stronger.

*And it hurts, it hurts, you don't know how to quit,*
*You yearn, and only take another hit,*
*Yet freedom's there, if only you will try;*
*Reach for the light before you have to die.*

Do you remember how it felt to be a child,
Before you learned the world is full of pain?
You've got to try to turn it back again,
To the time before it all got so defiled.

*And it hurts, it hurts, you don't know how to quit,*
*You yearn, and only take another hit,*
*Yet freedom's there, if only you will try;*
*Reach for the light before you have to die.*

*Hugh Smith*

# The Bucket Run

Shirley S . Tye

ON THE FIRST DAY OF SPRING, THE gentle April showers quickly turned into a heavy downpour. I felt secure with the knowledge that the roof and windows weren't leaking, and that power was flowing through the electrical wires. Everything had been working as designed. Everything was working fine—except the sump pump. It had seized during the night, leaving us with two inches of water on the basement floor.

My husband raced home from work with a new pump. Ah, nothing spells love in the county better than a new sump pump with a red bow on it. After the mess was cleaned up and the new pump installed, I felt confident that our water problems were solved.

A few weeks later, another rain storm hit. In my confidence, I sat and mocked the weather – that is, until the storm knocked out the electricity. Then in the dark, I bailed for three hours, puffing and panting as I lumbered up and down the basement stairs, keeping just ahead of the water pouring into the sump well. My darling husband again came to my rescue – this time with a sump pump alarm beautifully gift wrapped. He's such a romantic.

Nervously I watched the dark clouds gather into a thick angry mass and felt the cold wind pick up speed. I wondered about the batteries in the new sump pump alarm. Were they fresh? The answer came a few minutes later when the heavy clouds burst open and sheets of rain were pushed by strong winds that knocked out the electricity again. Yes, the batteries were working just fine, I thought as I watched our miniature poodle scramble under the bed to hide from the high pitched squeal of the alarm.

For the third time that year, I exercised with the water buckets. It was a breathless race to keep up with the flowing water. I bailed two buckets at a time from the sump, trudged up the basement stairs in my rubber boots, slouching water as I pushed my way out the front door. I stumbled onto the front lawn, letting the screen door bang shut behind me. I heaved the first bucket, lost my balance and slid face first into the slippery grass. Quickly I hopped to my feet and glanced around. Did the neighbours see that? I thought I saw the blinds sway in the house across the road. After a few runs up and down the basement stairs with the buckets, I got the swing motion down to rhythmic dance. Things were going pretty well. I was keeping up with the little Niagara that was pouring into the sump well. Then the wind increased speed.

As I was tossing the water from the second bucket, I heard a clunking, banging sound. I looked up to see the plastic bucket that I had just emptied bouncing down the driveway. Beside it ran our frightened miniature poodle. Apparently the door hadn't shut tight. I dashed after the two runaways. My feet slipped inside the rubber boots. The next thing I knew, I was running in my stocking feet down the muddy driveway, commanding the dog and the bucket to come back.

Neither one obeyed. I ran faster. Little stones began sticking to the bottom of my socks like tire studs giving me traction. The chase continued along the road for a few minutes before I managed to retrieve the two runaways. After that episode, I kept one foot in the empty bucket while pouring the water out of the other bucket, and I made sure the screen door closed tightly behind me.

After an hour of running back and forth with the buckets, I realized that my out-of-shape body wouldn't hold out much longer. I made a phone call to my husband at work and breathlessly said that I needed him to come home immediately. He was excited.

After he retrieved the fallen telephone, I explained that I wanted him to bring home a generator and a for sale sign. He must have misunderstood because instead of coming home with the items I had requested, he brought home a battery-operated sump pump. I suppose I should be grateful because it'll save me the hassle of bailing. Electricity goes out often in this neighbourhood, which means I'll have plenty of opportunity to test it. But, of course it only works when installed.

Now here I sit, six months later, with buckets at the ready.

# God Can Still Slay Giants

Geraldine Nicholas

MY CHILDREN GREW UP BEFORE the advent of *Veggie Tales**. But even back then children loved to hear Bible stories. The harrowing adventures and last minute escapes of courageous Bible characters were instant attention getters. Like Gideon who, following God's instructions, was not afraid to oust the cowards from his army and go into battle with only 300 brave men to face a formidable foe with an unusual combat strategy. Or Samson, the strong man who terrorized the Philistines and, even after being deceived by his devious wife, managed to die a hero. And the narrow escape stories of Daniel and the three Hebrew children. Or Jonah's ordeal in the belly of a whale.

At the top of the list is the story of David and Goliath. What child would not enjoy learning about a brave boy who, while soldiers cowered in fear, went out courageously to battle a despicable, taunting giant with only a slingshot and five smooth stones? And defeat him! Children need to know that God is powerful and can use the young and old to accomplish His purposes.

There are still plenty of giants around today. They have names like hate, prejudice, greed, illiteracy and poverty. These menacing monsters stomp recklessly, leaving a trail of chaos and hopelessness throughout the world. We all need to know that that God is bigger than our giants, and rather than cower in fear and timidity, we can be part of the solution.

So how can ordinary people like us make a difference? There are so many ways! Some distribute clothing to the poor or provide meals for the hungry. Others help immigrants with language study in their new surroundings. At Christmas time thousands of caring people fill shoe boxes with hygienic items, school supplies and toys for needy children all over the globe. Many people provide monthly support to a child or family with the hope it will make their life better. Thousands respond when natural disasters occur by offering themselves or resources to assist in the clean-up. Scores of doctors, dentists, nurses, builders and others pay their own travel expenses and donate their varied skills in third world countries.

A TV documentary told of an Ontario high school teacher who wanted to make a difference and challenged his students and community to help finance a water project in Guatemala. After two trips and considerable difficulty, ten wells were drilled and tens of thousands of children and their families have a clean source of water.

A team of 31 from Alberta (12 were young people), with the help of their local church, transported recycled playground equipment from the Edmonton area to Antigua, Guatemala where they built a playground to improve the quality of life for children there.

Dell and Marie Wergeland, along with an army of volunteers, load 40 foot containers from 'The Warehouse' – a place they rent in Victoria, British Columbia. Donations come in from all across Canada – bedding, school supplies, clothing, medical items, computers and many other reusable items. They are sent to places like Sudan, Tanzania, Nigeria and other third world countries. One shipment which included manual typewriters and other office equipment were used by a missionary in Africa to provide secretarial training to African women. As a result many of them were able to get jobs in government offices.

Motivated by compassion and a desire to serve, scores of men, women and young people are getting involved in a conspiracy of love that reaches around the world. It is amazing how God uses the generosity, kindness and courage of individuals to make a difference in the lives of others at home and abroad.

In these days of extreme world tension and conflict we need to remember that God can still slay giants. And He uses people who are willing not only to "love with words or tongue, but with actions…" (1 John 3:18 NIV)

I hope I never get too old to be motivated by the perilous journeys of Noah, Moses, the apostle Paul and others. They inspire hope in the face of hopelessness. These faith driven heroes seem fearless. The reason, of course, is that their confidence is in God, so as they do their part they can leave the result with Him. And so must we.

**Veggie Tales* is a children's animated video/DVD series that teaches timeless values and life lessons. Each one presents a nugget of truth rooted in Bible stories. *Veggie Tales* are available in many book stores. To find out more log on to http://www.bigidea.com.

# Including the Kitchen Sink

Glynis M. Belec

"FREE."

The tattered cardboard sign leaned precariously on the mottled green countertop resting at the edge of the driveway. Should a sudden breeze have happened along, the sign would have been history. Passersby would have been none the wiser.

Not wanting to miss a chance at a bargain, my frugal radar went on alert. I had spotted a slender gooseneck desk lamp next to the countertop.

"Hon, can we stop?"

My obliging hubby put his foot on the brake and pulled over.

"Do you see the sink?" he said.

"Sink?"

"There." He pointed at the stainless steel unit. "Isn't that similar to the one you wanted for the house?"

I could barely believe my eyes. I had seen the counter top from afar, but I hadn't noticed the sink.

Let me back up a little. About a month ago, my hubby and I received the devastating news from our landlord. He was apologetic about asking us to move, but he planned to include our lovely rented country property as part of a wage packet for his newly hired farmhand. Although he told us we had been model tenants over the years, that did nothing to soften the blow. Twice before we had put down roots, only to learn later on that each of these homes were to be sold. We were fed up with renting.

After a little cry, I started wondering about God's plan for us. Later that week, we felt a nudge to visit the bank. Plucking up the courage to do so, we prayed that our debt to income ratio was showing some improvement.

Something was brewing in the happy department. Before we knew it, all was well and the mortgage was a go. We would soon be building our very own home. No more renting. We made plans and I started looking through catalogues and online for ideas. The budget looked good. We promised each other we would be careful and keep our eye out for bargains.

As I leafed through a fancy catalogue, I noticed a lovely stainless steel sink unit: one smaller sink and a traditional one with an attached stainless steel draining board. Perfect. I dog-eared the catalogue and took it to show my hubby. He liked the sink. We put it on our "to buy" list.

To say that I was flabbergasted beyond explanation as I gazed at exactly the same sink now sitting on the side of the road a few days later, with a "free" sign on it, was no exaggeration. I looked heavenward and grinned.

We spoke to the girls as they pulled some more interesting items to the curb. Their father had recently passed away, so they told us they were clearing out his house and just wanted to get rid of everything. They insisted they did not want any money. They were thrilled that I was thrilled about my "new" sink. It sported a few paint flecks here and there and appeared a little grubby. Nothing that a little vim and vinegar wouldn't fix.

As we drove away with our sink and gooseneck lamp treasure, we were still in awe at our find. When we got it home, we removed the sink from the countertop and were surprised to discover the brand name was the same as we had seen in the catalogue and the sink was virtually unused. Not a mark on the plumbing. I dusted it, then got my pail, water and cleanser. Shortly it sparkled like a shiny new nickel.

I am still in awe at how God provides. It might only be a few hundred dollars cut from the budget, but every penny counts. Saving a few dollars makes me glad, but what pleases me more is the way God communicates in the everyday and how He really does care about the details.

Coincidence? Maybe. I'm thinking more along the lines of "God-incidence." Out of all the sinks in the world, what are the chances that I would find the very sink I had my heart set on sitting on the curb? He surely does provide everything we need - including the kitchen sink!

# A Flight of Faith and Freedom

Linda McCrae Tame

IT MUST HAVE BEEN HORRIBLE FOR him to see. Ryan, my son, was just 10 or 11 the day he witnessed a dear little bird being traumatized by our dog Andy. The bird struck the window, and Andy began taunting and terrorizing him by grasping him between his teeth; then releasing him to a feigned freedom. The fence was just close enough to hinder a winged escape, and it would send the helpless creature back to his tormentor again and again.

Ryan came to me in great distress. He is a compassionate person. I could see the anguish in his eyes and sense it from his heart.

"Oh mom, please come, there's a little bird out here that's hurt." We ran to the back yard, and there, lying on the ground, was this precious little bird, whose beak kept opening and closing as though it were calling out for help, yet there was no sound. I wondered to whom would he call? Do mother birds come and help their young? But this didn't appear to be a baby bird. Who would hear him, if he had voice? Do others from the flock stop their flight to aid one who is in need? I doubted that.

"He must be calling to God," I thought. "God hears from our hearts. God knows." Ryan lifted the anxious bundle of silently-squawking feathers and gently carried it to the picnic table.

"What can we do Mom?" he pleaded. "If he tries to fly away, he may fall again and be in worse trouble." We examined him and could see that his wing was broken or dislocated. The tiny body lay there, trembling under our strokes of comfort. His beak finally stopped its silent plea, and the little bird's body became limp, his breathing shallow.

"He has been through an ordeal, Ryan. He needs to rest, " I said. "Get a basket from the house. We'll place it over him, so the light can still shine through, but he will be protected." This seemed to satisfy Ryan at the moment.

Over lunch I wondered what to do. If he dies, my little boy will be so very sad.

"Father, you know all about this. We will trust you," I prayed. After lunch we went outside to check on our dear little feathered friend. He seemed much more settled and even tranquil. Looking through the openings in the basket we could see he was now standing and his wing seemed to have straightened. We were delighted, but now what should we do? If we let him go, it was possible he may try to fly, and if his wing was still weak, he might hurt himself even more; yet we couldn't keep him confined either.

"Ryan, it says in the bible that even a sparrow will not fall to the ground apart from the will of the Father. That means God is aware and He has a plan, a reason for this to have happened. Do you understand?"

"Yes, he nodded. "Let's ask God about this. We can't keep this little bird locked under the basket, or he'll die. We need to trust God to take care of him."

"Okay, " he responded warily.

"Father, thank you for allowing Ryan to discover this precious little bird of yours, so that he could offer help and comfort. Please heal his little wing. Please give him strength to fly safely again. Please look after him. We know that you are aware of his suffering, and we will accept whatever you do in this. Thank you Lord. Amen."

"Go ahead, honey, lift the basket." Ryan hesitated. I asked, "Can you trust God for the future of His own little bird?"

"Yes, I can, " he replied with conviction. He placed his gentle hands on the basket and carefully lifted it away. That sweet little bird gracefully lit into the air with a song of joy. God put a new song in his heart, and the wind beneath his wings. Ryan and I rejoiced! We praised God! We even cried and thanked the Lord, not only for giving flight and freedom to this little bird, but for the new song in our own hearts and the wind in the wings of our faith.

# One Hour Flight

We're often together
you and I busy going
somewhere
you with friends or the ipod
and I alone
the chauffeur

Now stalled on the tarmac you offer
one earbud to share
a ski movie with
your head on my shoulder
neck in a position
it will regret tomorrow

and I regret nothing
how could I have known
when we hit the ground running
that lightning delayed so many flights
struck so many schedules,
shredded plans for our long weekend

Movie over you dream breathe soft
warm head on my shoulder
held firm in place by my cheek
ear against the pulse
of lifeblood echoed
in your own

after a six hour wait covered
in the soot of closed spaces closer faces
one look in your feisty eyes
fragile at fifteen
I would not trade this
for the flight of the Concorde

*Joyce Harback*

# Where I'm From

I am from Ozarks, from Quaker Oats and hard work.
I am from the rough-and-tumble;

ill-fitting hand-me-down boots
unbuckled and dripping on the lino.

I am from the cicada's nighttime buzzing;
flowering mimosa and stifling humidity.

I am from singing grace and debating opinion,
from Frank and Eva and too many lives cut short.

I'm from the Show Me State, from singing and laughter,
warm cinnamon rolls and juicy watermelon.

From 8 brides for 7 brothers, the gifted grandpa,
and the dad who made an RV from a hearse.

I am from boxes of Kodak slides,
record albums piled in dusty corners,

the unpublished poem book, the praying mamma
and sticky caramel memories not yet unwrapped

*Joyce Harback*

# Comfort

Fixing our eyes upon Jesus
We do not sink in despair
Walking by faith through the darkness
His gentle hand guides us there.

While we are still in the chaos
Asking "Where do we go from here?"
He answers our heart's deepest longings:
"Follow me. You will see. Do not fear!"

For those who trust and obey Him
He rises with healing release.
And by the grace of our Savior,
Our hearts surrender to peace.

*Joyce Harback*

# Perhaps "Why?" Is the Wrong Question

For all the ways you are weakened
For all the days you are sore
For all the things you've been seeking
The Lord has given you more.

For all the words left unspoken
For all the times you feel lost
For all the nights you are broken
God paved the path to the cross.

In suffering there is a reason
A purpose for feeling alone
Your tears may last for a season
His arms will carry you home.

*Joyce Harback*

# Cassie

Marcia Lee Laycock

FOR AS LONG AS SHE COULD remember, Cassie had fallen asleep listening to the river sighing and whispering beneath her bedroom window. She had discovered if she laid her ear on one of the logs that made up the wall separating her room from the swirling current, the sound was clear, as though it were magnified. She would wrap her quilt around her and lay her slim body along the logs, and dream that she was part of the water, always moving in slim silver streaks, catching the light.

Her father had added her bedroom to the back of the cabin when she was a baby, newly weaned. He had added another room onto the side when her brother Andrew was born, and had started a room for Joshua, but Cassie had begged to have the baby in with her for a while. After all, she was ten and very reliable, and Josh had been so tiny, so very tiny. The crib was put under the other window in her room by the river, and the work on the last addition had gone slowly. Now, of course, it had been abandoned.

Cassie sat up, staring for a moment into the blackness, into the corner where she had seen the spider's web earlier that day. Then she remembered she had swept it away and cleaned the logs from floor to ceiling before getting into bed. Slowly she lay back down, covering her ears with her hands and rolling over to the edge, away from the wall, as far as she could without falling out. She fell back to sleep curled tightly into a ball, her hands still clamped over her ears.

As morning light spread across the floor of the bedroom, Cassie became aware of her tingling arm and the stiffness of her back and legs. Then she heard the river and slipped quickly from her bed, dressed and went into the kitchen. She began laying kindling in the stove's firebox, aware of her parents moving about in their bedroom. Her mother was first to appear, in a heavy housecoat and moccasin slippers trimmed with white rabbit fur. Cassie stared down at the slippers, remembering how she used to stroke Josh's cheek with the fur and how he squealed, tucking his chin down.

"Cass, we need water. Go fill a pail for me, will you?"

"But I'm lighting the stove."

"I'll do that. Your Dad will want his coffee."

Her mother pushed her gently toward the door as she spoke. Cassie tugged on a pair of heavy rubber boots, took a white plastic pail from the porch and pushed through the screen door. The sound of the river seemed to flow over her as she walked toward it, staring at the bottom of the pail gripped tightly in both hands. She followed the path automatically, stopping at the edge of the large smooth rock where she had so often dipped the pail into the river. In the heat of the summer she would sometimes lie on this rock, her cheek pressed to the cold stone, her hands trailing in the ice cold water. Now she stood trembling, staring down at the rush, the toes of her boots carefully placed just at the edge of the rock. She must have stood there for some time, unaware of anything but the swirling eddies and whirlpools a few inches beneath her feet, unaware of her father, standing behind her, watching.

He said her name softly and placed a large hand on her small shoulder. It trembled, then jerked back from his touch.

"It's all right. I'll get the water, Cass."

She dropped the pail and ran to the house, the heavy rubber boots thudding on hard-packed earth. When she reached the front door she stood for a while leaning heavily against it, her chest heaving. She stayed there until her father came with the pail, reached around her and opened the door without saying a word. Her mother looked up and seemed about to speak, but a glance at her husband made her turn back to the stove, her question unspoken.

Andrew charged in, breaking the silence. "What's for breakfast, Mom? I'm starved." He peered around his mother at the stove as he shoved his shirt-tail into his pants.

Jim Chambers laughed. "Are you ever anything else?"

Cassie watched the laughter in her father's eyes fade as he saw her watching him, and she quickly looked away. Her mother placed a plate of toast on the table and sat down as they all bowed their heads and waited for the usual blessing to be said. It was the custom at the morning meal to ask the blessing not only on the food but on the family, naming each one and asking for God's hand upon them. As Cassie listened, her father named each of them, speaking as though God were sitting there at the table, then he paused. Cassie clutched at her dress, waiting. "And Lord, be with little Josh too, and give us peace. Amen."

Cassie's hand trembled as she took a piece of toast from the plate. She didn't look up or speak as the others discussed the day ahead. She stared at the toast in front of her, remembering how they had laughed the first time they gave Josh peanut butter. He had made a face and licked the roof of his mouth several times, then grabbed a handful of the brown butter and smeared it over the tray of his high chair. Cassie turned suddenly from the table. The baby's high chair was gone from its place in the corner.

"What did you do with it?"

The tone of her voice caused everyone to jump. She continued to stare at the empty corner.

Jim sighed deeply. "We gave it away, Cassie, with the crib."

She turned back to the table, lifted the piece of toast from her plate, then put it back and stood up. "I'd better get ready for school."

Cassie found them in each other's arms when she returned to the kitchen. Her father stepped away and turned to her. "I have to take the truck into town this morning, Cass. Why don't you ride with me?"

"No. I want to take the bus."

"I'll go with you, Dad!" Andrew bounded into the kitchen, his books in disarray under his arm.

"O.K., son, let's go then."

Jim did not take his eyes from his daughter's averted face as he spoke, and as he turned to leave his shoulders sagged.

Cassie waited until she heard the truck rumble from the yard, then gathered her books and left the house. The morning was fresh with the first crisp touch of fall and Cassie found herself thinking impatiently of the winter. Winter would stop the river, seal it into a thick, silent slab of gray. Following the lane toward the road where the school bus would pick her up, she walked slowly, glancing now and then between the straight green trunks of the aspen trees. Now and then she caught the gleam of the water.

She stopped and listened, then put her books down carefully on the side of the road and plunged through the bush. She did not feel the wild rose bushes scratching at her legs, or the thick high-bush cranberry that slapped at her face, but she could hear the river getting louder, laughing louder, as she ran toward it.

Panting and disheveled, she reached the river bank, stooped and grabbed up a handful of stones, heaving them into the water. "I know you have him! Momma says he's with Jesus, but I know you have him!" She was whispering the words between clenched teeth as she threw stone after stone.

"Daddy said it was my fault, but it was you - you called him and he went to you. You took Josh away."

As she stooped to pick up another rock, a large black spider crawled out from under it. Cassie froze. Then she began to scream. She did not know she was screaming. She was staring at the spider, studying it the way she and her brother had studied that other spider on that other morning last spring.

It was a morning like this one, cool and bright with early spring sunshine. Andrew had noticed the spider first as it worked delicately, spinning a fine web between two small branches on the bush near their front door.

"Hey, Cass, come look at this!"

Cassie had Josh in her arms as she stepped into the yard. She quickly became entranced with the spider, watching as the insect skittered along the fine threads of the web that held the morning dew. Josh had begun to squirm and she put him down beside her, his small hand in hers. She became fascinated with the colors on the spider's body, the way it moved its spindly legs with such precision. She didn't notice when Joshua's small hand slipped from hers, nor hear his tiny bare feet as he padded along the path to the river.

They were still watching the spider when their mother called them for breakfast and Cassie had not noticed Josh was gone until she stepped back into the kitchen. They had all dashed back into the yard, calling his name, looking up and down the lane, thrashing through the bushes. Cassie was staring down the path to the river when her father caught her by the shoulders and began to shake her. "You were supposed to be watching him! Where did he go? Where did he go?" Her mother had come, finally, and pulled him away, leaving the girl silent and trembling.

Someone was shaking her now. Slowly she became aware of her mother's voice.

"Cassie, stop, please, stop it!" The voice sounded like

someone yelling beside the blaring whistle of a fast moving train. Slowly the whistle began to change into the wail of a human scream and finally she knew that it was her own. She stopped and stared for a moment into her mother's face.

"I'm sorry," she whispered, "I'm sorry." She let the stone slip from her hand and let her mother lead her along the river bank to the house.

They were still sitting on the couch, Cassie wrapped in a large quilt, crying quietly, when her father came home. Lynn met him at the door and Cassie could hear the murmur of their voices. Her father came and sat down beside her, slowly putting his arm around her. She stiffened beside him. They sat silently for some time. When Cassie finally looked into his face and saw that he too was crying, she sagged into him. "I'm sorry," she said again.

"I know, Cassie, I know. I should never have blamed you. I was in a panic and I just didn't know what to do. I know it wasn't your fault."

"But I should have been watching him!"

"So should I, and your mother, and Andrew. All of us, Cass, not just you, all of us."

Cassie crawled into her father's lap and lay there for a long time before asking one more question. "Will God forgive us, Daddy?"

She felt his strong arms tighten about her as he answered. "Oh, yes, my girl. He already has."

# Afterword: A History of the InScribe Christian Writer's Fellowship

*compiled from articles by Shirley Kolanchey and Elsie Montgomery*

A review of the history of ICWF brings to mind driving many miles to conferences and executive meetings, being at many venues, meeting and making new friends, and learning many new things about God and writing.

The Central Alberta Christian Writers (as it was originally called) began when a group of 12 writers from Alberta attended the Decision School of Christian Writing in Calgary in July 1979.

June Bevan, of Rocky Mountain House (she now lives in Kelowna, BC), suggested to the others that "we need to do something like this in Alberta." Sophie Thunell and Ruth Vikse agreed to help her. June became the first president, with Ruth and Sophie forming the executive committee. At first, there was a pastoral advisor, but this was eventually dropped as pastors were found to be too busy to make a long-term commitment.

The purpose was "to provide a vehicle for mutual support, stimulation and growth for Christian writers in Alberta." The main objective was to sponsor an annual conference. The first one was held November 8, 1980, at the Canadian Lutheran Bible Institute in Camrose, with a remarkable attendance of 66.

At the same venue the following year the attendance was 42, with 22 paid-up members (fee $15), and the name was changed to Alberta Christian Writers' Fellowship as writers began attending from all over the province. Early forms of advertising included interviews with the executive on CKRD-TV (Red Deer) and write-ups in local papers.

Subsequent fall conferences in the 1980s were held at Camp Kuriakos on Sylvan Lake, Lacombe Nazarene Church, Oriole Park Missionary Church in Red Deer, North American Baptist College (NABC) in Edmonton, and the Grey Nuns Regional Centre in Edmonton. In October 1989, the tenth anniversary of ACWF was marked at the Hospitality Inn in Calgary.

Presidents over the years have been June Bevan (1 year), Sophie Thunell (2), Alice Cundiff (1), Sophie Stark (7), Lavyne Osbak (1), Gerald Hankins (2), Elsie Montgomery (6), Marcia Laycock (5) Eunice Matchett (3), and Lisa Wojna (since fall 2008).

Each conference features a variety of workshop topics, including poetry, fiction, nonfiction and devotionals, depending on availability of leaders. Early keynote speakers included Rudy Wiebe and John Patrick Gillese. In 1987, when Maxine Hancock made the opening address at the NABC in Edmonton on the Friday evening, there were 125 in attendance. The membership increased from 32 that year to 98 in 1988.

The conferences were on Saturdays at first and then Friday evening was added. For several years, Wisemen's Way Bookstore from Camrose provided a display where members' books could be purchased.

The first writing contest deadline was June 30, 1983, and the judges were arranged by Alberta Culture. The yearly contest has been popular ever since, with judges being chosen from a variety of backgrounds. The number of entries have ranged from 37 in 1984 to more than 200 in 2000.

A home workshop was formed on September 15, 1986, at Barbara Mitchell's home. The latest count (see the list on the back of the *FellowScript* newsletter) shows 15 satellite groups meeting across Canada.

In 1983, Helena Brown, a retired Grade 1 teacher living in Didsbury, sent out the first *ACWF Newsletter.* It was a single page of two columns on one side, with a cartoon on the back and a space for the mailing address. She sent out 15 newsletters in all, finally reaching nine and a half pages, with her own homey comments, words of encouragement, scriptural quotations, and information about conferences and contests. From these humble beginnings (which served a useful purpose), the newsletter grew and grew to the present 28-44 page computer-produced edition, with several editors putting in hundreds of hours to get them done (the longest serving being Nathan Harms and Elsie Montgomery). In 1993, the name was changed from *ACWF Newsletter* to *FellowScript* in a contest won by Marion Jackson.

In the early 1990s, we met again at the Grey Nuns Regional Centre, twice at the Prairie Bible Institute (Three Hills) and in 1993 at the Star of the North Retreat Centre in St. Albert (with Janette Oke speaking on Friday evening and Marge and Bernard Palmer on Saturday). It was back to Camp Kuriakos for 1994 with Maxine Hancock and Phil Callaway.

On March 25, 1995, ACWF had a booth at the Book Fair at the Edmonton Convention Centre. The executive was ever on the lookout for a permanent location and on Sept. 29-30, 1995, we moved to King's University College in Edmonton (with Lorna Dueck as the plenary speaker). Conferences were held there until 2001 with most of the Friday evenings ending with a fun "coffee house" after the opening speaker.

Spring Workshops were added in April, 1990 and1991 at the Oriole Church in Red Deer, then at the New Sweden Mission near Wetaskiwin for three years. In 1996, the name was changed to Spring WorDshop and held every year to 2005 at Rocky Mountain College in Calgary. For writers in Southern

Alberta, it was more convenient than going to Edmonton. A Spring Literary Competition was included.

A major move was made in the fall of 1996 to expand ACWF across Canada, called ACWF-CanadaWide, and in 1999 it was renamed InScribe Christian Writers' Fellowship. The conferences and executive meetings are still held in Alberta.

In 1998, the Odes of March was initiated by Nathan Harms and Barbara Mitchell under the umbrella of ICWF, with poetry readings in bookstores and restaurants. In 2001, Nathan personally funded a poetry contest to coincide with readings, and the events moved out from the ICWF umbrella, although ICWF members continue to be very involved. By the spring of 2004, the Odes of March had been incorporated as a nonprofit organization called Utmost Christian Writers Foundation, sponsoring poetry contests with $8,000 in annual prizes and many other events including readings, gatherings, and the inauguration of an International Poet Laureate.

A necessary and important addition to the programs of ICWF has been the use of technology. In 1999, we registered our domain name as inscribe.org and posted a website. It has grown from a few pages to a large resource for writers.

After trying a discussion group of our own, which became cumbersome as the list of members grew, we turned to yahoo.com and created a listserv, letting Yahoo do the work of mailing each member's messages to every other member. This listserv is a good communication tool. We share questions, answers, successes, flub-ups, prayer requests, and friendly greetings with one another. We may never meet in person, yet consider our online friends true friends indeed.

For our 20th anniversary in 2000, Nathan Harms published an excellent book, *Companion,* to mark the occasion with history and photos, and members were encouraged to contribute one page about themselves. Four Alberta writers —Phil Callaway, Linda Hall, Maxine Hancock and Janette Oke—were the featured speakers, using the theme "Celebrate the Word." Since 2002, we have met each fall at the Providence Renewal Centre.

We also started using technology to record our Fall Conference speakers. Voice recorders smaller than a cell phone pick up every word said. Handouts are reproduced as .pdf files, and both are burned to CDs. Sometimes photographs are included, making this as close to being there as possible for those who cannot attend, or for those who want to review the workshops again after they get home.

In 2007, we began a blog at http://inscribewritersonline.blogspot.com. Blogs are normally online personal journals, but their use and description has expanded. The InScribe blog is a place where members can post short samples of their writing and get feedback from their peers or anyone who happens to find this online resource.

We also offer online courses. The first one was a course in writing poetry. We've also had courses in how to write devotionals and how to write Bible studies. In these courses, e-mail becomes the media of instruction and is also used by participants to submit their work for evaluation. The instructors may also choose to form a Yahoo group for the term of their course, making sure all students can experience this online classroom as they share and learn together.

God's blessing has been evident through ICWF and the Fellowship has become a widely recognized force in Christian writing. Members' publishing credits are often listed in the newsletter and the number of books being published is on the increase. To the dedicated executive members (eight or more annually) who have met in homes and restaurants over the years to put it all together, and to associate executives, we say thank you and God bless.

# Biographies

**Martha Toews Anderson**, founding member of InScribe Christian Writers Fellowship, started writing as a newspaper reporter while in high school. She has written feature articles, short stories, and devotionals, published in both trade and religious publications. She expects her first novel to be in print in the near future.

**Irene Bastian** resides and farms in the Foothills MD near Okotoks, AB. Current writing projects include reflections of God's handiwork and life lessons in farming and nature as well as the beginnings of a book based on her family's walk of faith as Irene's daughter struggles with a major health disorder.

As a freelance writer, author and private tutor, **Glynis M. Belec** has been happily writing for twenty years and has a particular passion to write for and about children. She has authored two children's books, written numerous short stories and has over 1000 magazine articles, newspaper columns, plays and devotions published. (http://www.inscribe.org/glynisbelec)

**Gwyneth Bell's** poetry has its roots in a deep love of nature, compassion for the sick and elderly, and the Christian faith. Poetry discovered Gwyneth rather late in life when she attended a workshop at an ICWF conference. She has enjoyed many conferences since then, and attended several courses at Grant MacEwan College and the University of Alberta.

**Dorothy Bentley** enjoys skiing and hiking with her husband, children, and Labradoodle in Alberta. She writes about them often in her Saturday TODAY column, and she is working on her first novel.

**Stephen T. Berg**, director of Development at Hope Mission, lives and works in Edmonton's inner-city. His book *Growing Hope—The Story of Edmonton's Hope Mission,* was published in 2010. A frequent contributor to the Edmonton Journal's Religion page, he writes on issues of social care and justice. Stephen is the 2009 recipient of the Waldo Ranson Spirit of Edmonton Award.

**Wayne Bos** joined InScribe in 1992. Several contest awards and numerous publications have followed. He has a BTh. from Prairie Bible College and a M.T.S. from Edmonton Baptist Seminary. He writes devotionals, non-fiction, fiction, and poetry. Wayne met his wife, Lois, at an InScribe retreat and married her in 2003.

**J. Paul Cooper** has been writing for the last fourteen years, and has had articles, essays and short stories published in newspapers, magazines and anthologies. He's the author of the young reader's novel, *Fluffy: A Cat's Tale* and a member of the Writers Guild of Alberta.

**Jan Cox** has published two devotionals, a number of articles in magazines and a Bible study. With the help of guest bloggers, she publishes a blog called *Under the Cover of Prayer* (http://underthe-coverofprayer.wordpress.com.) Jan lives in Haliburton, Ontario with her husband, Wayne. They have three children and four grandchildren.

**Janice L. Dick** is the author of three historical novels, dozens of book reviews and several short stories and inspirational pieces. Besides writing, she also does some editing, speaking and teaching. She lives with her husband on a farm in central Saskatchewan. Janice loves Jesus, her husband, their three married kids and their spouses, and their eight grandkids.

**Isabel Didriksen**, active volunteer, retired Home Care RN, wife, mother and grandmother, began writing about 1996. Poetry and short stories related to work and family have provided an outlet for emotions. Her desire is to share the message of God's grace and love through the gift of writing.

Retired teachers **L. Marie Enns** and husband Henry have four children, three children-in-law, and five grandchildren. Marie has written poetry for years and currently writes meditations for a local newspaper. She has published two books, and is in the process of publishing a compilation of her and her father's writings.

**Alvin G. Ens** is a writer of poetry, short fiction, family history and more. Just often enough he is published in magazines, anthologies and the web, wins contests and is short listed, and is told that his writings are enjoyed for him to want to continue writing.

**Sharon Espeseth**, a retired teacher living in Barrhead, Alberta has poems, stories, and essays published in various Christian and secular publications. Sharon participates in a local writer's group and belongs to InScribe. Her other joys include time with husband Hank, their adult children, grandchildren, and friends.

**Judith Frost** lives in Montreal with her husband, daughter and a Golden Doodle named Killarney. Her current passion besides poetry is learning about healing prayer. She also keeps busy quilting and as part of her church leadership team.

**Dr. Gerald Hankins** is a mountain-lover living in Canmore. He has devoted much of the time in his twilight years to writing articles, stories, poems and even books. A widower for almost a year, children and grandchildren are a source of joy and pleasure, as are hiking and photographing wildflowers. A pot-pourri of his thoughts, poems, tributes and experiences is due for publication some time before the end of 2010.

**Joyce Harback's** articles have appeared in the *Calgary Herald, City Light News* and *Rhubarb Magazine.* Her poem, Comfort, received honorable mention in the 2008 Christian Publishers Poetry Prize. She loves singing, photography, hiking and cloud-watching. She is married and has one son.

**Mary Haskett** has written two books and is working on two more. Her first award winning book, *Reverend Mother's Daughter*, won favourable reviews in Canada and the US. She has had many articles published and has been a regular contributor to her community's Christian paper as well as being founder of a critique group.

**Sheri Hathaway** works as a clerical assistant in Saskatoon. She has four grown children and two grandchildren. Writing human interest articles, children's stories and poetry, she has won several awards from InScribe's contests including the Barnabas Fellowship in 2004

**Evelyn Heffernan** is an award-winning poet, keynote speaker and workshop facilitator published across Canada and the United States. She has inspired writers groups, led post-partum support groups and addictions groups. She is now leading women's spirituality groups and women's healing circles. Visit Evelyn at www.sojournersmirror.com.

**Elaine Ingalls Hogg's** writing may be found in books, several anthologies and in an inspirational column she writes for the *Kings County Record*. She is a former winner of InScribe's Barnabas Fellowship award and has had stories included in more than a dozen anthologies, in magazines, newspapers, and on CBC radio. Elaine and her husband, Hugh, live in Sussex, NB.

**Marianne Jones** is a member of the League of Canadian Poets and was appointed International Christian Poet Laureate 2010-2012 by Utmost Christian Writers. She is the author of two poetry collections, *Here, on the Ground* and *Highway 17*. Her work has won numerous awards and appeared in many literary and Christian publications. She lives in Thunder Bay, Ontario.

**Janice Keats** is a freelance writer and speaker. Her passion is developing and teaching workshops on various Biblical Studies. She is a certified lay pastoral counselor and is presently employed in ministry. She is the author of *Poems of Inspiration and Occasion* and *A Journey to the Heart of Evangelism*.

**Shirley Kolanchey** is a life member of InScribe, and an *Edmonton Journal* retiree. She has enjoyed travelling across Canada, the U. S.,

Mexico, Europe, Far East, Hawaii, Egypt and Israel. Shirley was very active in sports, helped for years in Sunday School, and since retirement is still trying to find time to do more writing (mainly non-fiction).

**Marcia Lee Laycock** has won many awards for her work. Winner of the Best New Canadian Christian Author Award for her novel, *One Smooth Stone*, she has a second novel due to be released in the spring of 2011. The short story in this anthology was her first piece of writing to be published. Visit Marcia at www.vinemarc.com.

**Eunice Matchett** is an award winning author. Her short stories and articles have appeared in numerous Sunday School papers and other magazines. She is mom to five children and Grammy to eleven grandchildren. She lives with her three cats in Drayton Valley, Alberta.

**Elsie Montgomery** has published more than 2000 articles in magazines and newspapers, written Bible studies for 30+ years and teaches a distance learning course on that topic. She currently records daily devotional thoughts online. Elsie is also a wife, mother, grandmother, great grandmother, artist, and a quilter (not necessarily in that order).

**Eulene Hope Moores** hails from of Stony Plain, Alberta and seeks to create writings, including Letters of Hope on her weblog, that are motivated by Titus 2:3-5, to give to her readers inspiration from the Scriptures, and encouragement in the Christian Faith.

If there is one thing that **Pam Mytroen** loves more than writing, it's re-writing. The first draft of her romance novel is nearly finished and she can't wait to begin the revision (maybe it's the chocolate). She should also mention that she adores her husband Kel and their four children.

**Violet Nesdoly** freelances in several genres. She has been published in a variety of print and online publications and is an avid blogger. She lives in Langley, B.C. with her husband and is the mother of two adult children and a grandmother. Visit her on the web at www.violetnesdoly.com.

**Geraldine Nicholas** (Gerri) has many published items - articles, devotionals, short stories, poetry; has contributed to six books and written children's Sunday School curriculum. She served with her husband, Don, in pastoral ministry for 36 years. They have three grown children, six grandchildren, and now live in Sherwood Park, AB.

**Kimberley Payne** is a motivational speaker and author. Her writings relate to raising a family, pursuing a healthy lifestyle, and everyday experiences in building a relationship with God. Through her work, Kimberley hopes to inspire people to live their life to glorify God. You can visit her website at www.kimberleypayne.com.

**Cynthia Post** was a long-time member of InScribe as well as a talented artist. She self-published a volume of poetry and a novel. She resided in Olds, AB, with her husband, Bill.

**Susan Roberts Plett** writes poetry and prose from the home in Calgary, Alberta that she shares with one small dog, two medium-sized children and an adult sized husband. She has published poetry and prose in a variety of print and online publications and is currently seeking to hammer out her first novel.

**Barbara Quaale's** many adventures include sailing a tall ship, running a horse and carriage business, and competing in the Canadian Death Race in 2007. She currently resides in Alberta and has a passion for loud socks, heavy rains and large mugs of Earl Grey tea. *Santa Claws* is her first published work.

**Francis Ruiter** traveled to Canada via a troop ship to Halifax and continued by rail to Houston BC in 1948. From there he moved to Edmonton, eventually become a Life Insurance agent, until he became a left below-knee amputee, and started to write his memoirs.

**Ella Sailor's** passion is story telling. Both fiction and non-fiction roll easily from tongue or pen. She is a gifted author and speaker; holding a BA in Bible and Theology and a MA in Counseling. Ella enjoys memberships in The Word Guild and InScribe Christian Writers' Fellowship.

Married for 35 years, **Janet Seever** has two adult children and one grandchild. She is a writer and editor for Wycliffe Bible Translators in Calgary, Alta. and in her spare time occasionally writes articles for a church newspaper. Her inspirational stories have floated around the world on Internet.

**Linda Siebenga** is challenged and delighted that The Word gave us words; the dance of language and the creative possibilities of putting pen to paper. She is still geographically located west of Lacombe on a grain farm with her husband Jack, within twenty minutes of both sets of grandchildren. In the last five years she has also begun to put brush to canvas.

**Hugh Smith's** most gratifying literary accomplishment has been the publication of his critically acclaimed Hutterite novels *When Lightning Strikes* and *When the River Calls*. He has been a finalist for poetry in the $10,000 Tilden Canadian Literary Awards competition, and markets his popular comedy sketch materials through his enterprise, smith.comedy Press.

**Ruth L. Snyder** is a freelance writer who enjoys writing devotionals, articles, and stories. She is a member of the InScribe Christian Writer's Fellowship and an associate member of The Word Guild. Ruth lives in scenic northeastern Alberta with her husband and five young children. Contact Ruth at sun.beam3@yahoo.ca

**Sophie Stark's** interest in writing originally stemmed from lessons learned in an Alberta country school. She became an active member of Alberta Christian Writers' Fellowship in its early years and rarely missed a conference, often sharing her many skills. On the back of her poetry book, *Tableland*, Sophie said - "My poetry is meant to express my love for people, my devotion to God and my deep affection for this special province." It is also now her legacy.

**Linda McCrae Tame** is in love with life and has a storehouse of experience to share. After raising a family of five children, she is using her time now to explore adventures in the arts through travel and full-time university studies. A happy believer, Linda enjoys her faith.

**Shirley S. Tye** is a published writer and speaker/storyteller. Her writings have been published in periodicals, anthologies and websites. She has been a guest speaker as "Aunt Shirley" at retirement and nursing homes, mentally challenged adult groups and churches in Ontario and Mexico. (www.inscribe.org/auntshirley)

**Sulochana Vinayagamoorthy** is a freelance writer who has been published in many Christian magazines. She was the devotional columnist for Fellowscript for five years. Currently she resides in Southern California with her husband and is working on her first book. She also leads a writers' group for women in her church community.

**Elizabeth Volk** has been writing poetry since her early teen years. After becoming a Christian, she wrote a lot more because God gave her a lot more life to write about! She lives in southern Saskatchewan now (after being an Albertan for most of her life) with her husband, Larry, and their pet dog, Sebastian.

**Mary Waind** is a retired elementary school teacher-librarian who lives about three miles from First Line West and Side Road 11. She enjoys biking in the warm months, skating in the cold ones, and being part of the In-Service Intercession and Sunday School teams at Crossroads Community Church.

**Bonnie Way** is a freelance writer, editor and stay-at-home mom with two daughters. She has a BA in English and is currently back in school to pursue a BFA in creative writing. She enjoys hiking, biking and watching movies with her husband. You can find her online at http://thekoalabearwriter.blogspot.com.

A veteran journalist, **Robert White** got his start freelancing for the *Alberta Sonshine News*. He's written for mainstream and Christian publications and is currently the editor of the *ChristianWeek* Ontario. An ICWF member (then the ACWF) in the early 1980s, he placed third in the Devotional Writing category in 1983.

**Carmen Wise**, BA MEd, is a musician and teacher in Calgary. She loves to write and has had articles and stories published in professional journals, travel publications and literary magazines. She enjoys life with her husband Mike and her two dogs Sprite and Dino. Mike and Carmen recently became grandparents of wonder baby Zoe.

**Brenda Wood** is a motivational speaker known for her common-sense wisdom, sense of humour, and quirky comments. Her latest book is *Heartfelt, 366 Devotions for Common Sense Living.* Contact Brenda at: www.inscribe.org/brendawood

**Karyn Wynalda-Booth** currently oblates through a life of gardening, writing, and creating from her niche in Calgary, Alberta. Her nomadic ways have resulted in passport stamps, university degrees, jungle fever, photos and journals, and her race car Kiwi husband. This is her first published work and she is thrilled.

# InScribe Satellite Groups

**British Columbia**

Fraser Valley Christian Writers – Abbotsford
Contact: Alvin Ens – (604) 859-5171 – aiens@shaw.ca

Peace Christian Writer's Group – Taylor
Contact: Marnie Pohlman – wmpohlmann@hotmail.com

**Alberta**

Women Word Weavers – Barrhead
Contact: Sharon Espeseth – (780) 674-2461 – sewrites@telus.net

ICWF Northwest Edmonton Chapter –
Contact: Shirley Kolanchey – (780) 939-3317 – sjkolanchey@shaw.ca

ICWF Edmonton Chapter – Southeast Edmonton
Contact: Laurie Hanchard – (780) 465-1084 hanco@telus.net

ICWF Red Deer Chapter –
Contact: Marian Warkentin (403) 346-0134 – wark@shaw.ca

Ready Writers – Foremost
Contact: Craig Funston (403) 867-3033 – funfam@telus.net

South Calgary Writer's Group –
Contact: Joyce Harback (403) 279-4486 – harback@shaw.ca

**Saskatchewan**

His Imprint – Saskatoon
Contact: Ruth Keighley rkeighley@msn.com
The Gabbies – Assiniboia
Contact: Pam Mytroen (306) 642-4065 –
upward@sasktel.net

**Manitoba**

Manitoba Christian Writers Association – Winnipeg
Contact: Pat Gerbrandt – pageware_71@yahoo.ca

Swan Valley Christian Writers Guild – Swan River
Contact: Addy Oberlin – waltadio@mts.net

**Ontario**

Ready Writers–London
Contact: Mary Haskett – (519) 474-1419 –
marymhaskett@gmail.com

The Writer's Crucible – Peterborough & Kawartha Lakes
Contact: Kimberley Payne – (705) 944-2111

**Nova Scotia**

Metro Christian Writers – Halifax
Contact: Janet Sketchley – janet.sketchley@gmail.com

*This list of satellite groups for InScribe is current as of August 2010. For an updated list, please see the back of a recent issue of FellowScript.*